W9-AMN-816

COOL careers
for
girls

as

Environmentalists

Also in the same series

Cool Careers for Girls in Air & Space

Cool Careers for Girls with Animals

Cool Careers for Girls in Computers

Cool Careers for Girls in Construction

Cool Careers for Girls as Crime Solvers

Cool Careers for Girls in Engineering

Cool Careers for Girls in Food

Cool Careers for Girls in Health

Cool Careers for Girls in Law

Cool Careers for Girls in Performing Arts

Cool Careers for Girls in Sports

IMPACT PUBLICATIONS I

COOL
careers
for
girls

as
Environmentalists

CEEL PASTERNAK

EAU CLAIRE DISTRICT LIBRARY

T 124025

Copyright © 2002 by Ceel Pasternak. All rights reserved. Printed in the United States of America. No part of this book may be used or reproduced in any manner whatsoever without written permission of the publisher: IMPACT PUBLICATIONS, 9104-N Manassas Dr., Manassas Park, VA 20111, Fax 703/335-9486.

Liability/Warranty: The author and publisher have made every attempt to provide the reader with accurate information. However, given constant changes in the employment field, they make no claims that this information will remain accurate at the time of reading. Furthermore, this information is presented for information purposes only. The author and publisher make no claims that using this information will guarantee the reader a job. The author and publisher shall not be liable for any loss or damages incurred in the process of following the advice presented in this book.

Library of Congress Cataloging-in-Publication Data

Pasternak, Ceel, 1932-
    Cool careers for girls as environmentalists / Ceel Pasternak.
       p. cm.--(Cool careers for girls; 11)
    Includes bibliographical references and index.
    ISBN 1-57023-172-9 paper
    ISBN 1-57023-173-7 hardcover
    1. Environmental sciences--Vocational guidance. 2.Women environmentalists--United States. I. Title. II. Series.

    GE60 .P37 2001
    363.7'0023--dc21

                                                        2001039394

Publisher: For information on Impact Publications, including current and forthcoming publications, authors, press kits, bookstore, and submission requirements, visit Impact's Web site: www.impactpublications.com

Publicity/Rights: For information on publicity, author interviews, and subsidiary rights, contact the Public Relations and Marketing Department: Tel. 703/361-7300 or Fax 703/335-9486.

Sales/Distribution: All paperback bookstore sales are handled through Impact's trade distributor: National Book Network, 15200 NBN Way, Blue Ridge Summit, PA 17214, Tel. 1-800-462-6420. All other sales and distribution inquiries should be directed to the publisher: Sales Department, IMPACT PUBLICATIONS, 9104-N Manassas Dr., Manassas Park, VA 20111-5211, Tel. 703/361-7300, Fax 703/335-9486, or E-mail: coolcareers@impactpublications.com

Book design by Guenet Abraham
Desktopped by C. M. Grafik

Thanks to Cindy Heil for her professional support and encouragement, especially help with writing.

Contents

Honda Distinguished Scholar in Transportation, University of California, Davis and Berkeley campuses

Environmental issues such as global warming, creation of deserts, loss of forests, loss of species, ozone depletion above the earth, and water and air pollution are very real. Each has a negative effect on our long-term health and welfare. Our daily lives and actions are closely interconnected with the environment. Indeed, our individual actions—collectively—have a huge impact on the earth both positively and negatively. Most environmental problems are connected to population and economic growth, using up our resources, and pollution resulting from the production and disposal of goods that support our daily lives.

You are probably reading this book because you are curious about whether you can make a difference in the environment and what career path might appeal to you. As you might expect, an environmental career is extremely rewarding, but it takes time, dedication, and education. The earlier you start exploring this exciting area, the better. You have a lot to consider:

• What environmental issues concern you the most?

• Do you need more information about particular areas?

• What subjects (biology, math, chemistry, writing, art) do you like the most and want to pursue further?

• Are you interested in working on a local, regional, national, or international level?

• What career tracks seem most interesting to you (government, industry, academia, grassroots-local, or nonprofit)?

Early on, I decided to focus on an environmental career, and now I have over ten years' experience on a wide range of issues. I have always felt closely connected with the environment and had a great desire to make a difference. So, I became involved with environmental projects after I finished my undergraduate (four-year college) degree. I explored many different options—I worked as a consultant to the U.S. Environmental Protection Agency and the U.S. Department of Energy, in an environmental nonprofit organization, and as a university researcher. This helped me identify a niche that was perfect for me: transportation and the environment.

I had a strong interest in research, so I pursued a Ph.D. degree in ecology, focusing on technology management and the environmental impact of transportation (autos and trains, primarily). At present, I am a research scientist at the University of California, leading several innovative transportation projects to help reduce pollution. They use advanced technologies such as electronic and wireless communication systems and low emission vehicles. I also direct a new research center focused on identifying new mobility solutions for the future such as CarLink: A Smart Carsharing System (a shared-use vehicle service that links clean cars to transit through the Internet and global positioning systems), which are both socially and environmentally beneficial.

Ecology—my area of expertise—is the study of complex interactions among organisms and the environment. In ecology, we learn that many species often respond to the environment by making the best possible use of their resources (food, shelter), filling their own unique niche space. Similarly, you, too, can start to identify the environmental niche or career path that best suits you. This book provides a great overview to get you started on your journey.

U.S. ENVIRONMENTAL MOVEMENT: GOOD STUFF TO KNOW

Before jumping into the career profiles in this book, you might find a brief overview of the U.S. environmental movement quite helpful. In fact, one of the first things I did early in my career was to learn more about the movement, its key events, its literature, and the people—environmentalists, scientists, politicians, regulators, and activists worldwide. (Some of these pioneers are mentioned in short stories throughout the book under the heading Groundbreakers.)

• In the late 19th century, John Muir wrote about his great love of the wilderness, which ultimately led him to launch the first major conservation efforts to protect natural areas such as Yosemite National Park in California.

• In 1949, Aldo Leopold, in his book, *A Sand County Almanac*, expanded our environmental vision to include the important role humans play in the natural world.

• In 1962, Rachel Carson's *Silent Spring* inspired revolutionary changes in governmental policy toward the environment. While this book highlighted the impact of chemicals on the environment, it also awakened concern about other negative environmental impacts such as energy use, auto emissions, and logging.

• In 1970, there were several exciting developments: the First Earth Day celebration on April 22, 1970; passage of the National Environmental Policy Act (an umbrella regulation that covers analysis of all environmental impacts prior to approving major new projects such as building factories or dams); adoption of the Clean Air Act; ban of the pesticide dichloro-diphenyl-trichloroethane (DDT, a cancer-causing chemical); and formation of the U.S. Environmental Protection Agency.

• In 1972, the Clean Water Act was passed.

• In 1973, E. F. Schumacher's *Small Is Beautiful* was published. This important book focused on the need for towns and cities to be more sensitive to the environment, resource use, and natural growth limits in their development. Also, the Endangered Species Act was passed.

- In 1974, the Safe Drinking Water and Toxic Substances Control Acts (pesticides and toxic chemicals) were adopted.

- In 1976, the Resource Conservation and Recovery Act (RCRA) was passed (waste management from "cradle-to-grave").

- In 1980, the Comprehensive Environmental Response, Compensation, and Liability Act was adopted (also known as Superfund, to remedy sites contaminated before RCRA).

- In the mid-1980s, the Clean Water Act was updated, and the Montreal Protocol was adopted (reduction of chlorofluorocarbons, or CFCs, which lead to depletion of the ozone layer in the sky).

- In the 1990s, the Clean Air Act was updated and the Energy Policy Act adopted. Furthermore, the Earth Summit in Rio de Janeiro, Brazil, and the United Nations Climate Change Meeting in Kyoto, Japan, were held on global climate change.

Throughout my career, I have worked with many of the regulations mentioned above as well as several others that I did not list. Many environmental jobs will involve working either directly with these laws or indirectly to develop technologies that help result in less pollution.

FINDING YOUR WAY

In this book, several career tracks are explored. They range from wildlife breeding to fuel cell technology development. These exciting careers cover environmental areas such as air, water, land, ecosystems, insects, animals, plants, and toxins. Some of the women profiled here made a deci-sion to become an environmentalist when they were girls and some much later. Their jobs represent a rainbow of areas—research, teaching, government, industry, and self-employment. Not surprisingly, their educational backgrounds also vary, ranging from a high school education, to advanced degrees, to self-taught; all include continuous learning.

Each story will provide you with an understanding of a typical day on the job, educational requirements, challenges and rewards, salaries, and employment opportunities. You will also find a checklist with clues about what personality types and lifestyles are most suitable to a particular job. In the final chapter, the women profiled offer advice on what you can do now. You'll find recommendations on books to read and where to find further information.

After you read this book, I hope you will continue to think about cool careers in the environment. Here are some suggestions as you start your exploration:

- Identify a role model and ask her to help you prepare for your career.

- Research websites, read suggested books, and contact organizations for more information about student programs and scholarships.

- Test the waters early through volunteering or with a summer job, if possible.

Write papers about different environmental topics as part of your class work and write letters to the editor of your local newspaper.

The world is yours! Enjoy it.

COOL careers

for girls

as Environmentalists

Robin R. Sears
Robin R. Sears

Graduate Fellow, Institute of Economic Botany, The New York Botanical Garden, Bronx, NY

Major in Botany, minor in Cultural Anthropology; master's degree in Forestry, Yale University, New Haven, CT; graduate student, Center for Environmental Research and Conservation, Columbia University, NY

Sustainable Forestry and Agriculture

Botanist

The Forest is Her Classroom

In a small rural farm area on the Amazon River in Peru, South America, Robin Sears is doing research. She is working on her Ph.D. degree in Ecology and Evolutionary Biology. Her passion is forest ecology, tree/forest management, and farming systems.

"It is so exciting to be right on the Amazon River, working with people who survive on what they grow and hunt!"

When Robin is there, she lives with a rural family. She spends her time measuring trees, taking inventory of the different species of trees in this tropical area, studying the different plants and crops, and conducting interviews with farmers about their systems. Robin came to the area near Iquitos, Peru, in the Amazon, with her Columbia University professor, who

Graduate Student
Fellowship and work-study salary pay living expenses
Research and travel expenses paid through various grants

ROBIN'S CAREER PATH

introduced her to the people he knows and to the forests and farms.

"He arranged for me to stay with a family that could feed and care for me, then, after a week, he left me with my notebook and equipment (duct tape, measuring tapes, first-aid kit, sample bag, and camera). Every day I work with the two local field assistants I hired. They are familiar with the peo-

plants. I talk with the farmers, who are very good at what they are doing, to learn about their systems and how they work. I'm especially interested in how the farmers use the trees."

Robin spends nonworking time just talking with the people—while at a local soccer game or washing clothes at the river—exchanging ideas, listening, and making suggestions.

> My professor arranged for me to stay with a family that could feed and care for me, then left me after a week with just my notebook and equipment.

ple, the trees, and the crops. They help me as I take notes about the many different species of trees and identify the

"My goal is to learn enough so that I will be able to look at a farming system or forest, assess which sites are

8

more suitable for managing trees, and be able to make recommendations about the type and number of trees and where to plant them. These farmers in Amazonia are very clever and know a lot. I learn a great deal from them. I can also teach them some things about the forest and trees from a scientific perspective after analyzing or testing their methods by doing experiments. For instance, because I am able to travel more than the farmers, I am in a position to share information with them from other parts of Amazonia. The more experience I have, the more I may be able to help the environment."

Robin has taken field trips to Brazil, Ecuador, Costa Rica, and Mexico following her two interests—the outdoors and science. "I have parallel passions. I want to be out wandering forests, climbing mountains, paddling boats, and I want to be part of the scientific world. I've found a career that lets me do both."

Early Interest in Science

Robin's interest in science began while she was growing up in rural western Massachusetts. Her father is a marine biologist and a professor who took Robin along with his students on field trips. "Growing up, I played in swamps, fields, the forest, and at the sea coast. I loved being outdoors. Because of the way I think, rationally and logically, I have many questions about things around me. That's my passion for science."

Robin's mother is a "fabulous gardener. She has a spiritual connection

ROBIN'S CAREER PATH

Gets joint fellowship—
Columbia University and
The New York Botanical
Garden

Takes several field trips to
South America working
on thesis

to nature. I get my wonder—that nature is wonderful—from my mom."

In junior high school, Robin had good teachers. She discovered she could have a good time with science and biology. "My father came to class as a guest speaker and made seaweed pudding. That started me on the path to the fabulous field of ethnobotany, people's use of plants."

The word botany refers to plant life, and ethno refers to people, a cultural group. So ethnobotany is about people's use of plants. Ethnobotanists study things such as how the Cherokee Indians use plants in their medicine; how tropical people use palm leaves as roofing material; and even how they use forest fruits for juices.

Seizing Opportunities

Robin's study of ethnobotany became a matter of seizing opportunities. Few students at the University of Massachusetts at Amherst were interested in the subject. "There were no real classes offered, so I had to pursue my interest elsewhere."

Robin was in the honors program at college, which allowed her to do a senior thesis. She found a program through the School for Field Studies, arranged a grant from her department, and went to the Amazon area of Ecuador, South America. There she took a one-month field study course on the Ecuadorian Amazon and ethnobotany, then spent five months studying people's house gardens in other parts of the country for her project. "That experience started my passion for tropical peoples and tropical ecosystems."

In preparation for the field study, Robin and a friend spent six weeks with her friend's parents in Costa Rica learning to speak Spanish.

After graduating college, Robin took three years off from school and followed her adventure-seeking nature. "I had a great job as a house painter, which paid well and gave me off-season time to take outdoor-adventure trips. I spent one year in Washington state as a sea kayaking guide. There I lived on Orcas Island. While it was great, I found I missed the academic life, the science."

Robin had kept in touch with former professors, who encouraged her

CAREER CHECKLIST ✓

You'll like this job if you ...

- Are passionate about the outdoors

- Have curiosity and want answers to your questions

- Can adapt to different climates and very different types of people

- Are fearless in learning languages

- Are also cautious, but open to experiencing new places and different peoples

- Don't mind 'roughing it'

to pursue her interest in ethnobotany. When one told her about an upcoming field study trip to Mexico, she returned to the Northeast and took this opportunity to return to science. "After that Mexico trip in 1994, I entered Yale's School of Forestry and Environmental Studies to get my master's degree. I spent three months in Brazil to gather information for my thesis and fell in love with the Amazon rainforest. That's when my interest shifted from ethnobotany to forest resource management and farming—sustainable agriculture and forestry."

field. I heard about a new program at Columbia University, and I decided to pursue my doctorate degree there."

Fellowships and Grants and Travel

Robin applied for and got a joint fellowship (which pays her living expenses) from Columbia University and The New York Botanical Garden. Her office is at the Garden, in the Institute of Economic Botany. As part of her work study, she helps the scientists with their research and works in

I'm fearless about learning a language;

I blurt it out; I have no shame.

With her master's degree completed, Robin started her first job in science at the IUCN—World Conservation Union in Switzerland. "I learned a lot in this large international institution dedicated to nature conservation. I enjoyed the work and living overseas but found I didn't want to be in an office, I'd rather be out in the

the herbarium (where dried plant specimens are mounted and systematically arranged for reference). She also has to work as a teaching assistant two semesters. (In a tropical ecology class, she and her students spent ten days on a field trip in Mexico.)

As a graduate fellow, working on her doctoral project, Robin spends time in the field and time in New York City. "I spend a lot of time going to field sites—the Amazon, the German Black Forest, the New England forests—and measuring trees, taking inventories, studying different species, doing interviews." When Robin's home in her New York apartment, she spends time in the library researching what is currently known, writing papers, meeting with professors, reading, attending conferences, and networking with other scientists and students with similar interests. "Occasionally I will collect plant specimens in the field and take them to the herbarium to verify their identity."

What's Next?

"Whenever there is an opportunity to go to the field, I take it. I get my name out there, talk at conferences, let it be known that I'm passionate about being in the field. I have research grants that will pay for all of my research expenses. I spent a lot of time last year preparing seven proposals, from which I won four different grants."

Robin has lots of ideas about what she may do when she gets her doctoral degree. "I am concerned about forests everywhere, and particularly in my native New England. Political awareness as well as scientific curiosity drives my research questions. While I enjoy spending time in other cultures, in exotic environments, I may seek a postdoc position working in New England. I also want a balanced life that will leave time for my other passions—bike touring, outdoor adventures, attending the opera, reading novels."

EAU CLAIRE DISTRICT LIBRARY

Mary Jayne Churchill

Mary Jayne Churchill

Animal Naturalist, Western North Carolina Nature Center, Asheville, NC

Endangered Species Red Wolf Breeding
Animal Naturalist

Life with Wild Wolves

Mary Jayne Churchill is like a female Dr. Dolittle, the storybook doctor who can talk to and understand animals. "The fun part of my job is getting to know the animals as individuals—getting to see each animal's personality—and their getting to know me. We have a relationship ... an understanding with each other. I've had a rapport with animals all my life. I believe it's not something you learn; you're born with it."

When one of the Nature Center's cougars, Valerie, seemed ill, Mary Jayne got on all fours, facing Valerie, and communicated with her mind, heart, and senses. When Valerie 'told' her what was wrong, her breathing, Mary Jayne got medical help. The next time Mary Jayne saw her, Valerie

Animal Keeper
Part time, $7 to $8 per hour

Animal Naturalist
Full time, salary $23,000 a year plus benefits

MARY JAYNE'S CAREER PATH

Rides horses
▼ soon as she
learns to walk

Raises sheep
▼ in the Ozarks

Travels with
▼ military stepfathe

bounced out of her house, lay on her back, looked up at Mary Jayne, and 'smiled' at her in thanks.

As an animal naturalist at the Western North Carolina (WNC) Nature Center, Mary Jayne cares for the cougars, bobcats, gray wolves, and red wolves who live there. She also spends some time with small mammals like otters and birds of prey. "A lot of the things I do for this job are just like what you do at home for your animals—feeding and watering them, looking after their health, cleaning their homes."

When one of Mary Jayne's animals needs medical attention, she usually stays with the animal while it's being treated and takes care of it during recovery. When the two red wolf puppies were born in April 2000, Mary Jayne provided hands-on care for their first two weeks of life to weigh and medicate them. While the breeding program calls for very limited human contact with wolves, handling the newborn pups is the exception. "Red wolf puppies are prone to staph infections. The belief is that this infection comes from hairline scratches on their pads and tummies where there is no fur. The scratches come from the floor of the wooden boxes they live in,

Graduates high
school in Florida

Becomes medical
transcriber, has farm

Moves to North
Carolina, works
at hospital

even though we put lots of clean straw in their box to lower the chance for scratches. So, we apply a topical antibiotic to those areas to prevent infection." By caring for red wolves, Mary Jayne is not only doing a job she loves, she is part of a national program to save red wolves and return them to the wild.

An Extinct Species

"Red wolves were one of the most extinct species—their numbers got down to 14—because of disease, habitat destruction, and predator-control programs. Then they started inbreeding with coyotes." To try to save them from extinction, the U.S. Fish and Wildlife Service captured the remaining purebred red wolves. (They determined whether the wolves were purebred by studying their DNA and x-rays of their bone structure.) The 14 purebred wolves were found mainly in the southeastern United States, but they were placed in captivity in various locations throughout the country for breeding. Point Defiance Zoo, Tacoma, Washington, was the first captive-breeding location. The WNC Nature Center is one of now 38 breeding locations.

"Why is it so important to get red wolves back out there? First, to keep the species from becoming extinct. Second, to restore the ecosystem to what it was when red wolves occupied it. By doing this, we are preserving our environment."

Unlike timber wolves, red wolves are more solitary and do not form packs. This and their smaller size make them the natural predator of smaller animals like rodents and make

MARY JAYNE'S CAREER PATH

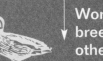

Works part time
with animals at
Nature Center

Works full time with
breeding program,
other wild animals

them good prospects for reintroduction to the wild. "Without their natural predator, the wolf, these smaller animals can overpopulate and die of starvation or become pests, because the diseased and weaker animals are not culled out (killed by the wolf and so removed from the population)."

Red wolves have already been reintroduced at the Alligator River Refuge in eastern North Carolina, on property donated by the Prudential Insurance Company. "This has been the most successful reintroduction. But, now, coyote inbreeding has become a problem there. One plan being considered is to capture the coyotes in a refuge and sterilize them. Coyotes have few predators. They're opportunist and adapt very well to civilization, so they're often a problem for people." Red wolf reintroduction at

Cades Cove, in the Great Smoky Mountains of eastern Tennessee, was not successful. "None of the puppies survived. I think they just didn't have enough to eat. It just didn't work." So red wolves have been removed from that location.

Mary Jayne's work and how she is helping to make a difference have been widely recognized. She wrote an

article about the successful effort to breed red wolves at the Nature Center in order to save them from extinction and restore them to the wild, and the American Association of Zoo Keepers published it in their journal, which has an international readership.

Caring for Red Wolves

Mary Jayne enters the red wolves' habitat every day, twice a day, to take a head count, feed and water them, and keep their home clean. "They stay away from me because they're shy. They're still very wild, even though this breeding pair (and their puppies) have been in captivity all their lives. We want to keep them wild because, at some point, the puppies may go into the wild. So, we don't want them to learn to be around people."

One time frame when the adult wolves did not avoid Mary Jayne was when she had to remove the puppies to medicate them. "Sadie, the red wolf mom, is a first-time mom and a good mom. She was good about letting me

CAREER CHECKLIST ✓

You'll like this job if you ...

- Have a real love of animals

- Are concerned about saving a species

- Like working outdoors

- Are disciplined

- Are easygoing, quiet, and soft-spoken (since wild animals are shy and scare easily)

- Are sensitive to the needs of animals

handle the puppies because both wolves know me and are more relaxed around me than others, but I couldn't have gone to other captive-breeding facilities. None have gone into the wild." Wolves selected for restoration

Half of what I do here is educating the public. You'd be surprised how many people don't know what a goat or sheep looks like, much less a wild animal.

do it alone. One time I was alone, and I startled one puppy when I reached for it, so it let out a yelp. Both parents ran right toward me when that happened. The hair on the father's back was standing up. I knew that they were just being good parents, but I didn't go into their habitat alone again to medicate the pups."

The U.S. Fish and Wildlife Service decides when the puppies are old enough to be separated from their parents. So far, no puppies younger than two years old have been removed. "Because the gene pool of our wolves is so good, all of our puppies

to the wild are placed in an area known as an acclimation pen for one year. "These wolves are used to people feeding them. They get dry dog food and zoo meat. Sometimes we get a pre-killed rabbit, but unless they get a squirrel on their own, they have never hunted." In the acclimation pen, the wolves are first given road kill to develop their taste for wild game. Then live, wild prey is gradually placed in the pen so the wolves learn to hunt. "Mom and dad aren't there, so the pups learn this on their own. The hunting instinct really kicks in."

Animals, Animals, Animals

"Animals have always been the most favorite thing in my life." And horses have always been in Mary Jayne's life. She started riding horses as soon as she could walk. Her stepfather was in the military, so she traveled a lot during childhood and lived in the Philippine Islands and Okinawa, Japan. She also lived in Florida, where she was born and has spent most of her life. "My favorite place is where I lived when I was five years old—the Ozark Mountains. My mother, my sister, and I lived in a three-room ranch house that had electricity but no indoor plumbing. We had 54 acres of land, and we raised sheep. I enjoyed raising sheep. We had a pair of standard-bred collies to help us herd the sheep." As an adult in Trenton, Florida, Mary Jayne owned a ten-acre portion of a large farm that was a winter training ground for standard-bred race horses—trotters and pacers.

When she was a girl, Mary Jayne had no idea about what she wanted

GROUNDBREAKERS
Champion of Chimpanzees

Jane Goodall (born 1934), has spent years in Tanzania, East Africa, on the shores of Lake Tanganyika studying chimpanzee behavior and social relations in the wild. Her scientific discoveries laid the foundation for all future primate studies.

She was fascinated with animals at an early age, read about them, and dreamed of living like Tarzan and Dr. Dolittle and writing about living with animals. In 1957, when in Kenya, she met the famed anthropologist Dr. Louis Leakey, who chose her to begin the pioneering study of wild chimpanzees.

She founded the Jane Goodall Institute in 1977 to provide ongoing support for field research. Today the Maryland-based organization has offices in Austria, Canada, China, England, Germany, Holland, Italy, South Africa, Taiwan, and Tanzania. Among its programs are education for young people, chimpanzee research centers, a program that studies chimpanzees in zoos and other captive settings, and chimpanzee sanctuaries where orphaned chimpanzees are provided with long-term care and rehabilitation.

Source: Jane Goodall Institute, P.O. Box 14890, Silver Spring, MD 20911-4890; Web site: www.janegoodall.org

to be when she grew up. "I wish I had been one of those children who knew what they wanted to be. I went through this stage where I wanted to be a vet, until I learned how much school and money are needed. I had it set in my mind that animals were always just for hobbies, until this job."

After high school, Mary Jayne took a medical transcription course (typing medical reports from recordings, usually made by doctors, so they can be printed) at Santa Fe Community College in Gainesville, Florida. "I was very interested in medical terminology. I lived in the country where I had my 'hobby' farm with many different animals, including a guinea pig named Winston Churchill. I commuted to the hospital in Gainesville where I worked. Medical transcription became my full-time career and gave me independence and freedom. It allowed me to work second shift (afternoon through evening), so I had all morning to ride my horse and do my chores. As it turns out, that background helped me tremendously with this job, because a lot of the diseases animals get are also diseases people get." During her medical transcription career, Mary Jayne did part-time work that involved animals, usually pet-sitting for horses while their owners were away.

From Hobby to Job

As a teenager, Mary Jayne had vacationed in western North Carolina with her family. In 1987, the mountains lured her back permanently. She moved to Candler, near Asheville, and continued with her medical transcription career at Mission St. Joseph's Hospital. Her office was in a basement, and she missed the outdoors. So, Mary Jayne began visiting the Nature Center to get outdoors. She got to know some of the workers there, and in 1995 she accepted a part-time job.

"Although I had no formal animal training from school, I had a lot of experience from my hobby farms." She began by working in the barn, caring for farm animals, one day a week and working with wild animals two days a week, and she switched to part-time work at the hospital. Then, one day, the Nature Center offered her a full-time position. Mary Jayne left the barn work and began full-time work with wild animals. "I really like working with the wild animals. When you work at the barn, you must stay there. But working with the wild animals gives me 40 acres to move in. Freedom is very important to me."

To prepare for her new job, Mary Jayne read as much as she could. "We have wonderful resources here, including fact sheets for all the animals. Those fact sheets contain a wealth of knowledge." Mary Jayne enjoys educating the public about the animals. "I sit out front in the pavilion to answer questions whenever I get a chance."

Mary Jayne, a county employee, works from 8:30 a.m. to 5:00 p.m., Thursday through Monday, and she gets one hour for lunch. She wears comfortable clothes for her outdoor work. Her employer provides paid vacation and sick leave, insurance, a retirement plan, and other benefits. Mary Jayne, who is divorced, owns her own home. She vacations at the beach and in Florida to visit family and friends. Although she doesn't own a horse now, she still rides. She also enjoys hiking, going to movies, and creative writing. "I fish and used to hunt, but now I just do target shooting."

Christi Theis

Christi Theis

Research Analyst, High Altitude Emissions Laboratory, Honda R & D Americas, Inc., Denver, CO; and **Honda Facilities Manager**, California Fuel Cell Partnership, West Sacramento, CA

Major in Psychology; master's degree in Environmental Policy and Management, University of Denver, CO

Clean Air—
Automobile Emissions
Facilities Manager

Focused on the Car of the Near Future

The car of the future is very much in Christi Theis's present. She has even driven it.

Christi, a research analyst for Honda R & D Americas, Inc., is the Honda facilities manager for a special project involving eight car manufacturers that are developing vehicles that use fuel cell technology. It is called the California Fuel Cell Partnership.

"Imagine a stack of fuel cells in the car that generate the power to run the car. There's no battery needed. A fuel cell is fueled with hydrogen and air. The fuel cell has a thin layer of material called a membrane, which allows the positive hydrogen ions to pass through it but not the electrons (which are negatively charged particles). The negative electrons travel

Research Analyst
Salary range from $45,000 to $55,000 a year

CHRISTI'S CAREER PATH

Grows up
on a farm

Graduates college,
works in psychology
with adolescents

Does office w
at emissions
laboratory

around the membrane creating electricity. That electricity is used to power the motor of the vehicle. Electricity is produced in the vehicle instead of being stored in a battery, so you do not have to 'plug in' the car and recharge a battery."

After the positive hydrogen ions pass through the membrane they combine with the oxygen in the air, which makes water. Water is the only emission that comes out of the exhaust, so there are no harmful substances to pollute the air. There is no CO_2 (carbon dioxide).

"This is such a clean process, and hydrogen is a naturally occurring abundant resource; it only makes sense to use it. Our job here is to educate people about this technology and demonstrate how the cars perform on the road—show how they work and how safe they are." (These cars are different from the Honda and Toyota "hybrid" cars now on the market that have a gasoline and electric motor combination.)

A People Person

"The thing I love most about my job is the people. I work with a huge, diverse set of people, both in Honda and with the partnership. A lot of the Honda people come from Japan. I've been to Japan to learn more about the technology. I can speak a little Japanese, but they have studied English since grade school. When they come to the United States, part of their job experience is to practice speaking, so we speak English."

In this partnership of auto manufacturers, fuel providers, government

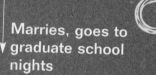

Marries, goes to
graduate school
nights

Earns degree in
environmental policy
and management

Divorces,
promoted to
research analyst

agencies, technology companies, and transit agencies, many of the people are from other countries—Germany, Korea, England, The Netherlands—and from different corporate cultures. "It's an amazing group, all these people working together."

worked with. I watch, see what they're doing, ask questions, and they explain. My technical knowledge is not real high, but it's good enough to help the people and to manage the office."

As facilities manager, Christi has many responsibilities. Her office is in

Our job here is to educate people about this technology and demonstrate how the cars perform on the road.

"I have a basic background in science, and I've read a lot. But I learn from everyone I meet. Talking with people who have already learned what you want to know is a good way to learn. I learn from engineers I've

the Honda section of a very large building that opened in November 2000. In eight separate work bays, the tech teams work on the cars. Every morning, Christi sits in on a meeting with the Honda tech team as they go

CHRISTI'S CAREER PATH

Travels to Japan, studies language, marries again

Takes management job at fuel cell partnership

over what they did the day before, any problems that came up, and what is scheduled for that day.

"I also spend a lot of my time in meetings with members of the partnership. I'm safety team leader—involved in setting up a safe environment for this facility. With so many different entities and cultures, both country and company, arriving at one safety plan that all will agree to is quite a challenge. I set up the meetings, send information, and do the minutes."

"I'm a member of the Working Group, which has at least one member from each partnership. This group actually planned the building, how it would be set up, how the demonstration program for the vehicles would work. One big challenging project was working with the fuel providers to plan a refueling station, where the cars are fueled with hydrogen. The hydrogen is shipped here in liquid form, then converted to a compressed gas. The fuel hoses, similar to natural gas fuel hoses, must be

One big challenging project was planning and building a refueling station, where the cars are fueled with hydrogen.

locked to the car's tank opening so no air gets in."

A big part of Christi's job is talking to visitors and showing them around. She usually wears dress pants, often with a jacket (unless she knows she is going to stay in her office, then she wears jeans). The main office is open to the public. It has displays (prepared by the partnership's communication people) explaining the partnership and how the different technologies work. "Part of my job is to take people into the Honda work bay, explain the development of the car, and answer questions."

Schools frequently bring students for a tour of the building, and the students often get to ride in a car. Christi got to drive a car around the building for a media event, to demonstrate how easy it is. "Now, I'm putting together presentations for elementary and high school students, to help them understand what is involved here." Christi has spoken in front of many groups, giving presentations on the Honda car and presentations for members of the partnership about current work and

CAREER CHECKLIST ✓

You'll like this job if you ...

- Are comfortable with all types of people
- Are interested in new ideas
- Are interested in learning from different cultures, different people
- Are not judgmental, have an open mind
- Are patient
- Can pay attention to detail
- Can handle many different tasks

future plans (like how 'gas' stations will be able to refuel these cars with hydrogen). "This didn't come naturally. I'm a shy person. But I learned to do it when I had to do a lot of presentations before groups in graduate school. The more presentations you give, the easier it is."

A Long Commute

Although Christi spends most of her time at the job in California, she still has her research analyst job at Honda's High Altitude Emissions Laboratory in Denver, Colorado. "I have reports and things to do for that office. I've recently hired an assistant in California, and I'm training her to take over some of my work."

While in California, Christi stays in a furnished apartment with maid service, which the company pays for, and she gets money for her meals. She travels home to Denver every weekend to be with her husband, Michael, and occasionally takes extra days to go in to work at the Denver lab.

Christi is a native Coloradoan. She grew up on a farm in Greeley, the youngest of eight children. "I admired my brothers and sisters and wanted to be like them. I thought for a while that I wanted to join the Peace Corps because my sister did, but I changed my mind. It wasn't until high school that I decided what I wanted to do. The mother of one of my best friends was a clinical psychologist. She was a single mom, raising three children and making a living. I admired her and decided to go to college and major in psychology."

Making a Living

When Christi graduated from Colorado State University, she worked in the field of psychology with emotionally disturbed adolescents. "It was very rewarding work, but very difficult, and it didn't pay very much. I was on my own and had to make a living, and that wasn't happening. I decided to take a break—just take a regular job temporarily while deciding what to do." That temporary job turned into her career.

It was the time of the United States's new standards for car emissions and the newly passed Clean Air Act. Because of Denver's location in the Rocky Mountains, several car com-

GROUNDBREAKERS
Started a Movement

When the book *Silent Spring* appeared in 1962, it alerted the world to the hazard of environmental poisoning. Its author, Rachel Carson (1907-1964), "an accomplished scientist, an expert on pesticides, and a woman of conscience," courageously stood up for her beliefs that synthetic chemical pesticides were putting the future of life on earth at risk and that government and industry should and could change what was happening.

A writer and trained zoologist, Carson joined the U.S. Fish and Wildlife Service in Washington to work on their publications. She wrote three books about the sea, becoming nationally known in 1951 for the bestseller *The Sea Around Us,* which opened up scientific knowledge about the oceans to the layperson.

She was by nature a shy woman, but became a crusader when an aerial spraying of DDT killed the birds in a friend's bird sanctuary. She began to investigate the effects of pesticides on the chain of life. Carson persevered through the storm of controversy and abuse that her book created, but did not live to see the eventual banning of DDT in 1970. The environmental movement carries on the work she began.

The organization founded in her name serves as an international clearinghouse for information on toxic substances and pesticides—Rachel Carson Council, Inc., 8940 Jones Mill Rd., Chevy Chase, MD 20815; (301) 652-1877.

Sources: National Women's Hall of Fame, Web site: www.greatwomen.org; Biography *Rachel Carson* by Linda Lear. (1997). New York: Henry Holt, 1997.

panies built laboratories there to do research. There's a big difference in how a car performs at high altitudes and the emissions that it puts out compared to sea level. "I got a job as an administrative assistant, though I could barely type. I did general office work and planned to be there only two years, but I became really interested in clean air technology."

"I grew up on a farm and took for granted the value of being surrounded by nature, growing up in a clean environment. Then I moved to Denver, living in the heart of the city. I remember one morning I was up at 5 a.m. and smelled the air. It was incredibly sweet and clean—but, an hour later, it smelled like exhaust. I knew then that this is the area where I wanted to work. I want people to smell that clean, fresh air all the time."

Doing Extra Work

Christi wanted to do more than her office duties, so she began reading, searching for the latest efforts in clean air technology. "Our staff was small, and our management was in California. So I'd write short reports or forward articles that I'd run across to my boss. I wanted to broaden my job. Sometimes I'd get feedback, so I kept at it. During this time I went to school at night at the University of Denver. After four years, I earned my master's degree in Environmental Policy and Management. I was promoted to research analyst."

As a research analyst, Christi got more involved in the science of reducing auto emissions. She attended conferences and wrote reports on the new information presented. To help develop the Honda vehicles, she performed comparison tests on vehicles from other companies. She also supported test teams from Japan that would test in Colorado or drive the ve-

I'm very appreciative; I've developed myself from a young girl who couldn't type to facilities manager."

I grew up on a farm and took for granted the value of being surrounded by nature, living in a clean environment.

hicles across the country to California or Ohio. Making sure the vehicles can perform well in extreme climates took Christi to places like Death Valley, California, in the summer and Minnesota in the winter.

"I met a lot of the company people—from Japan, from our Ohio and California offices—who came to visit the Denver laboratory. I'm not sure how I was chosen for the facilities manager job, but I think these people put in a good word for me. I felt qualified because I'd started at a secretarial position, and I've learned what it takes to put together and run an office. That's my job here in California.

When Christi is not working, she enjoys snowshoeing, canoeing with her husband, and hiking with her dogs Piper, Grady, and Keesha. "I love being in the mountains. As a farmer's daughter, I also have a knack for gardening and enjoy cooking the fresh vegetables from my garden."

Christina Uranowski

Christina Uranowski

Ecological Consultant and Owner, Wet Bound Consulting,
Tarpon Springs, FL

Major in Biology; master's degree in Botany, University of
South Florida, Tampa

Ecosystems—
Riverine Wetlands
Biologist

Her Research Protects Wetlands

"You have to give up some things to go back to school when you're older. It's much more difficult." Christina Uranowski didn't know that she wanted to be a wetland biologist and ecological consultant until 15 years after she graduated high school. But today she knows that she was right to change her career. "My work is my love. I can't believe I get paid for doing this!"

What Wetlands Do; Why We Value Them

Christina has been working on a model that shows what the riverine wetlands in west-central Florida do—how they function. (It is called the Hydrogeo-morphic Methodology for Measuring

Biologist
With BS degree: Salary range from $25,000 to $35,000
With MS degree: Salary range from $35,000 to, with experience, $70,000

Biologist Consultant, Private
Private consultants bid on jobs usually for a set price, which they figure according to any project costs they will incur, adding in the cost of the hours they believe they will have to work at the project, equipment, travel, and supplies. Average hourly charges vary. Average yearly income ranges from $40,000 to $70,000.

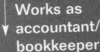

Wetland Functions.) "Riverine wetlands are the areas next to rivers that hold water when the river has overflowed its banks. Wetlands store water both above and below ground. The trees and other vegetation there slow the speed of the water as it moves above ground, and the water below ground moves slowly through the soil as it reaches the river channel. Wetlands have porous sandy soil, allowing floodwaters to seep through the sand and slowly reenter the rivers, rather than flowing rapidly to flood with damaging currents."

Wetlands do other things: Provide habitats for animals and communities for native plants (plants that naturally grow there), transport organic carbon (decaying plant and animal material), provide aquatic food webs downstream, and remove or clean up toxins transported in the water.

"That's what wetlands do, and we value what wetlands do. By storing water from an over-bank flood, the wetland helps prevent people's property downstream from being flood-damaged."

Wetlands also purify the water. "When water overflows a river's banks, the particles it contains (sediments, toxins, nutrients) drop out into the

Studies mangrove
forests with mentor

Works for
consulting firm

Starts ecological
consulting
business

wetland. The waffling effect of the vegetation separates these particles from the water. The particles drop to the soil and are recycled. Toxins are detoxified as the water filters through the soil, and the plants absorb many of the elements in the water. When the water returns to the river, it is purified."

Writes National Guidelines

Christina was doing this work for the U.S. Army Corps of Engineers (COE). She was awarded a contract based on earlier completed work. Part of her responsibility was to write a guidebook. "I used a guidebook for the riverine wetlands of Kentucky to develop the protocol for Florida's wetlands. I recruited a team of experts, and together we determined the functions for west-central Florida riverine wetlands. Florida's wetland systems are very different from Kentucky's, so we made a lot of changes."

The guidebook is a national document, and Christina taught two training sessions for its users. "The guidebooks are regional. Florida is divided into water management districts, and we had to determine where to establish our sampling. We decided to use the southwestern Florida water management district. I chose student interns and hired student assistants. We traveled all over the district and chose wetland sites that ranged from those already highly affected by development to those that are still pristine (natural, clean, undeveloped). We had 36 sites with three sampling plots within each site. The size of each sampling plot was .04 hectares. We took

CHRISTINA'S CAREER PATH

Develops riverine
wetland model

Marries
Craig

photographs at each site. We identified and measured each tree and counted all the shrubs within each plot. We identified all of the ground cover within a six-square-meter area of each sampling plot. We identified characteristics of each river—meandering (winding), wetland topography (terrain), soils and landscape features. This took about one year. The entire project took three years."

"There are larger rivers farther north, so there is a larger sampling area in that region. In west-central Florida the rivers are smaller and the floodplains are not as extensive as those in northern Florida. Riverine wetland types are extremely diverse. Places (hydric hammocks) are found where freshwater springs rise up in the river. Forested swamps are found where the elevation is low and

> A lot of what I have to do is specifically describe each type of wetland. My work is my love. I can't believe I get paid for doing this!

Christina found it difficult to find the right sites in Florida's southwestern water management district.

the river has a direct connection to the wetland. Bottomland hardwood forests are somewhere in between these two types, with slightly higher elevations, channel cuts in the levees, and with or without springs. In west-central Florida, all three types can be found occurring together, side by side. But a number of land managers didn't know the difference between the types, so I made many survey trips before making many of the assessment trips. As a result, I have described the specifics of each wetland type according to the landscape features, water source, and water direction."

People, like road builders and land developers, who are going to do something that will affect the bottomland hardwood forests of Florida will use Christina's guidebook. "This book will help them determine whether the site they want to develop is a high-quality site or a low-quality site. If they have to disturb the wetland, the book will help them choose the best place to do that and what wetland functions will be lost. This procedure is more scientifically based than the impact assessment they now use, where no measurements are taken."

CAREER CHECKLIST ✓

You'll like this job if you ...

- Like to be outdoors, love nature
- Like science and math
- Enjoy working both in the field and in the lab
- Want to help ecosystems
- Aren't afraid to ask questions
- Can work alone or on a team
- Pay attention to details

Controlling Exotic Plants

Another part of Christina's consultant work is to identify and recommend ways to control exotic plants—plants that do not naturally grow in a habitat but are brought into this country from foreign lands. People, birds, animals, or wind spread the seeds from one area into all types of habitats. "Florida has a big problem with exotic vegetation. I work with the exotic plants that grow on the edge of or inside wetlands, like the Brazilian pepper tree or the Australian pine, and some vines and ferns. They don't belong there and cause huge environmental degradation."

Christina has been involved in mapping—showing where exotic plants are growing in the public lands of the Florida Keys. "Exotic plants reduce the biological diversity, spread very quickly, and remove the natural vegetation that provides a home and food for the animals who live in the habitat." Christina's identification of the exotics is critical to the way they must be removed. "For just one or two trees, you can spray an herbicide around the base of the tree, then remove it when it dies. But in south Florida, there are forests of exotic trees, and they are very expensive to remove. There, aerial spraying is required." Because removal is so expensive, Christina recommends which area of exotic plants should be removed first when there are several forests of exotic plants on one large property. Critical and sensitive habitats should be considered as priority removal areas first.

Inspired by Her Parents

Christina grew up in Wilkes-Barre, Pennsylvania. Her parents' families came there from Poland and Lithuania. They brought with them an appreciation for the beauty of nature, and Christina's parents inspired that appreciation in their children. "Every weekend and all summer, they would take us to a natural area—a creek, the mountains, horseback riding. We never swam in a pool, only in streams and lakes. I had a lot of quiet times, alone, in the woods, and I really enjoyed it."

When Christina graduated high school in 1971, young women were encouraged to marry and have children, not to pursue careers. "I had no mentors, and I didn't have much inspiration to do anything else, but, deep inside, I wanted more."

Christina took an executive secretary job at a local construction company. She also did their bookkeeping, payroll, and estimating. She did this job for 15 years. During the mid-1980s, when she asked for a raise in pay, "They told me to get married. Then, about two weeks later, a man whose wife had just had a baby got an automatic raise. Some time after that, my boss hired a Certified Public Accoun-

tant (CPA) to do what I had been doing, and he asked me to train the CPA. I was told that I would no longer work independently, as I had for all those years. I decided then to leave and move to either Florida or California. I had never visited California, but I had visited friends in Tampa, Florida, and knew that I loved it, so I chose Florida."

Back to School

When Christina joined her friends in Tampa, she got a job, found a place to live, and enrolled at the University of South Florida (USF) to study. She attended USF part time, while working full time, for two years. Then she decided to become a full-time student to finish the additional years needed for

We value what wetlands do for us;

they prevent disastrous floods from destroying

our homes and businesses.

her bachelor's degree. She applied for student loans, scholarships, and grants to support herself so she could go to school full time. "The CPA left that Pennsylvania construction company less than one year after I moved. They offered me a raise to come back. I turned it down."

After receiving her bachelor's degree, Christina decided to continue going to school full time for her master's degree. At USF, Christina met Dr. Clinton Dawes, who became her major professor, mentor, and inspiration for protecting wetlands. Dr. Dawes hired Christina as a research assistant while she was studying for her master's degree. "That covered the basic cost of living, but I did take a few student loans to help."

Finding the Work She Loves

Christina immediately began working with Dr. Dawes in the marine environment, studying mangroves (trees that adapted to grow along tidal shores with root systems that are often underwater). She did her master's thesis on mangrove algae. "I was constantly under the microscope, but I loved it!" Christina still works with Dr. Dawes. They have published several papers together and are currently working on a paper about the mangrove forests on the west coast of Florida.

Dr. Joseph Simon was Christina's invertebrate zoology professor, and he, too, inspired her. "His course was very difficult, but he told us exactly what he expected of us. His lectures were very stimulating, interesting, and exciting."

After graduating, Christina accepted a job with a consulting firm. "I learned a lot about the practical application of what I had learned academically and in the lab—what's happening regarding restoration. For example, I worked on transplanting sea grass, restoring ecosystems, and learned about the negative impact that the huge influx of people moving to Florida is having on the ecosystem."

She was already doing some work for herself and was teaching at a community college when the Florida Department of Transportation awarded a project to the community college, and Christina decided to leave the consulting firm to head this project as principal investigator. That project led to increased funding from the COE to complete the riverine wetlands model project for publication.

Home on an 8,000 Acre Preserve

About four years ago, while working on the wetlands project, Christina toured the Cypress Dome property near Tarpon Springs. There she met Craig Huegel, the manager who showed her the property and later became her husband. Craig is now the Pinellas County land manager and manages the county's environmentally sensitive land. He and Christina live on the 8,000-acre Brooker Creek Preserve.

Christina enjoys fishing and scuba diving, and with all of the property she lives on, she has lots of room to pursue gardening. She likes to grow herbs, vegetables, and orchids. She has begun to study yoga. She and Craig enjoy going to concerts presented by folk singers. She mentors for the Association for Women in Science, and she is an adjunct professor at Hillsborough Community college, teaching biology and environmental sciences.

Debbie Lewis

Debbie Lewis

Energy Consultant, Owner, RnR Engineering, Wimberley, TX

Major in Electrical Engineering

Renewable Energy—Wind

Electrical Engineer

Putting the Wind to Work

Working outdoors, building wind power plants is Debbie Lewis's idea of the most fun job. She was in charge of a three-year project of the Lower Colorado River Authority (LCRA) to bring wind-producing energy to Texas. As the utility's project leader she coordinated all the various parts of the project.

The first step involved contract negotiations to choose the people who would build and operate the wind plants. Phase two involved negotiating with other utilities to purchase or handle the power. During phase three Debbie worked with the groups within LCRA, such as the board of directors for approval, the men in charge of monitoring the generation plants, the men designing the transmission sys-

Electrical Engineer
Beginning salary: $36,000
Experienced: $60,000 and up

Consultant: Paid by the hour $100 to $250
Also, consultants bid on jobs for a set price, which they figure according to any project costs they will incur, adding in the cost of the hours they believe they will have to work at the project and other expenses, such as software or travel.

DEBBIE'S CAREER PATH

Enjoys outdoors, Campfire Girls Graduates as electrical engineer Works in Albuquerque, NM then Austin, TX

tem, and the entire administrative department (insurance, accounting, and public relations). Phase four involved permits and monitoring construction by the developer, plus lots of accounting. The final phase was the grand

ing the project, which upon review got the project an award from the U.S. Department of Energy—National Award for Energy Efficiency and Renewable Energy, Best in Category, Utility Technology.

Campfire Girls are very involved in Native American lore and their love of the environment. So, I was constantly exposed to a love of the environment.

opening, informing the public, and properly acknowledging those within LCRA who worked so hard to get the project done.

When the project was completed in 1996, Debbie wrote a paper describ-

As the project came to an end, Debbie thought about her future work. "I knew that I'd never be as happy as I was during those three years. I realized I could never sit in an office and not build wind power plants."

Gets job with Lower
Colorado River Authority

Marries
Lamont

Assigned wind
power project
leader

Debbie quit her job, took time to evaluate what she wanted to do, and decided to work as an energy consultant. Now she chooses the jobs she likes and works in the renewable energy field. (Renewable energy sources are those that can be replaced by natural ecological cycles, like wind, sun, and water. Oil and natural gas are not renewable sources because the supplies are limited and can't be replaced by a natural cycle.)

The Texas renewable energy mandate, to build 2,000 megawatts of renewable energy between 2000 and 2010, has clients demanding Debbie's expertise. Debbie now studies the best places to put more wind power plants, matching the windy areas with access to the power grid. She is also working to develop biomass energy projects, which turn agricultural products into electricity. And she is educating the public on pollution issues related to electricity generation.

A Campfire Girl

Debbie's parents instilled a love of the outdoors in their four children. "I grew up in Mount Prospect, Illinois, a Chicago suburb. We spent time sailing, camping, and walking in the woods. My mother told us it was our job to pick up trash we found, even though it wasn't ours. She and her friend worked to get recycling started in the 1960s." They became Campfire Girls leaders and persuaded the community to recycle. "We'd drive through the neighborhood on trash night and pick up the newspapers of neighbors who weren't recycling them." Debbie was a Campfire Girl from second grade through high school. "Campfire Girls are very involved in Native American lore and their love of the environment. So, I was constantly exposed to a love of the environment."

Debbie's father was "an electrical gadget genius." He influenced her interest in technology. "I was an introvert who liked to play with creative toys and to build things. I had friends

and enjoyed them one-on-one, but I didn't like large groups."

Debbie loved school and knows the importance of having good teachers. "When I encountered a negative math teacher, my mother, who taught math and science before marriage, spoke with school officials about the teacher's attitude. I had an excellent chemistry teacher and a very creative physics teacher who involved his students in hands-on experiments. They sparked my interest in physical science."

Not a Nerdy Engineer

Debbie's ACT (American College Testing) scores for math and science were high. Those scores, along with her love of the environment, prompted her to enroll in Southern Illinois University's environmental engineering program. But Debbie didn't concentrate on only engineering courses. "I took a lot of sociology courses to get the sociological perspective. I think they helped me, so I wasn't thought of as the nerdy engineer. I know they helped me understand how to work on a team and how to get things accomplished with people. Later in my career, I realized a course in political science would have helped me because, in the end, politics run everything."

"The most beneficial non-engineering course I took was oral interpretation of literature. We had to give presentations in front of our peers. Later in my career, when I had to give presentations to hundreds of people, this course helped me to be comfortable and to translate what I was reading and thinking into words that people could understand and appreciate."

Debbie transferred to the University of Texas at Austin and changed her major to electrical engineering, because, in 1980, a lot of environmental engineering was waste-water related, which didn't interest her.

CAREER CHECKLIST ✓

You'll like this job if you …

Love the environment

Are a problem-solver

Like math and science

Are creative and like to build things

Want to work with engineers

Like and respect men, comfortable in a 'man's world'

"Renewable energy wasn't a big thing then, and pollution control wasn't a consideration, either. And I love Austin, which is an environmentally sensitive city."

Debbie studied semiconductor devices and materials because she was interested in lasers and solar panels. When she graduated in 1983, she "chose BDM, a company in Albuquerque, New Mexico, because they had solar panels on their roof, and they were somewhat involved in energy development."

Though Debbie moved to Albuquerque, her heart was back in Austin with Lamont, whom she met in college and who later became her husband. "I flew to Austin every chance I had for one and one-half years." When a BDM subsidiary in Austin had a job opening, she transferred and moved back to Austin. She developed a database for geologists and did some instrumentation work.

Time to Rethink Her Worklife

When Debbie was in her late 20s, the company she was working for laid everyone off. Debbie took time off to decide who she wanted to be and what she really cared about. "I decided I wanted a career that fit with my value system. This included my love of the environment."

Debbie rewrote her résumé for each job she applied for. "I spent hours at the library and talked with people who worked at each company to learn about the company. These efforts got me interviews and employment offers from semiconductor and electrical engineering companies. But I was really interested in working for the Lower

Colorado River Authority. In addition to being a utility, LCRA was a steward of the environment, responsible for the lake and dam systems and parks development in central Texas."

Although Debbie's formal education did not include the study of power, "I had a basic understanding of power; it comes naturally from studying physics and electrical engineering. Plus, a lot of what I did for BDM was computer-oriented, so I knew my way around a computer and had written lots of software. LCRA hired me to be a computer systems analyst and to develop software that would analyze the transmission system. I had the right combination of electrical knowledge and computer experience, and I let them know that by researching LCRA and rewriting my résumé when I applied for a job there."

Getting the Wind Power Project

While working at LCRA, Debbie volunteered and networked with the Texas Solar Energy Society and made sure that her colleagues knew she was interested in renewable energy, which was gaining national interest in the early 1990s. "Renewable energy wasn't in my department. So, it was a struggle, but the department involved in renewable energy knew I was interested and sent me to conferences. I let everyone know that if I didn't get the work I was interested in, I was out of there. If there's a position they need to fill in renewable energy, let me do it!"

They listened to Debbie, and the most important day of her career came at a renewable energy conference. There, the guest speaker was the person who used to run LCRA and had left to develop Sacramento's solar energy program. "He's an incredible fighter for renewable energy and the environment. After he finished speaking, he motioned me to follow him. I was nervous. I had never met him when he was at LCRA; I was just a little worker at this enormous utility company. We wore name tags that had where we worked, and he knew I was there. He asked me how things were going at LCRA. I'm honest; I told

> Of all the things I did, I most enjoyed talking about the wind power project to people to help them understand it.

him 'Not very well. They just can't get the ball rolling [for renewable energy development].'" During this conference, Debbie was also on her honeymoon with Lamont. "It was a good week all around!"

"Within a month, there was a rumor at LCRA that there might be a wind power project, which would be the first in Texas. I learned later that my conversation with this man is what got the wind power project going."

A Good Boss

The LCRA department head for the wind power project selected Debbie to be the project leader, so she transferred from transmission planning. "The wind power project was the pet political project of the time, but very difficult to get started, especially with other utility companies. It was so new and different that it was considered awkward in Texas. Nobody else had gone beyond the research and development scale."

Then, Debbie learned that she was pregnant with her first son. "I worried that an old-school utility company might not give me the project leader job because I was pregnant, but the man who picked me for the job was incredible. He said 'Well, so what? You're pregnant, but you're good. We need you, and I want you. You can do it.' And I did do it. It was this boss's confidence in me that got me through it."

Debbie worked 50- and 60-hour weeks, putting in time at work and at home. She took six weeks off for the birth of her son, Colton, and then went back to work. Debbie and Lamont's neighbor provided child care for

Colton. "But when she wasn't able to do it or Colton was sick, Lamont took care of him, because, very often, I was in west Texas putting up a wind plant, or in negotiations with other utility companies, or I had to be out of town for other reasons concerning the project. Lamont's help and support are what saved me."

During the project, Debbie enjoyed speaking at chapters of the Institute of Electrical Engineers throughout Texas, the Audubon Society, other utility companies, local groups, and the Chambers of Commerce in small towns. "Of all the things I did, I most enjoyed talking about the project to people to help them understand it. And one of the best moments was receiving the DOE award."

A Balanced Life

"Since leaving LCRA, and after having my second child (a son, Colin), I could have worked as much as I wanted to. But I made a conscious decision not to. We had saved money and didn't trap ourselves with material possessions. So when the time to make a change in my life came, I could buy the computers and software I needed to start my own business and work at home." To stay connected to the energy business world, which is very important for getting her clients, Debbie stayed involved with the groups that support renewable energy. "I always paid my dues for my professional engineering license, even when I didn't have as much income."

Now, Debbie chooses her projects so she can balance her time for work; her time with her children, which includes attending their school activities; and her time to volunteer. "I participate in the Hays County Master Naturalist Program, which is a volunteer outreach program." To join this program, Debbie had to attend classes to become certified. Through this program, Debbie educates her neighbors about choices they can make to help their local environment. "The decisions I made early in my career have given me the freedom to do what I want now, and now I can give back."

Ann Bauman

Owner and Partner, Millennia Group, LLC, Austin, TX

Green Technologies and Products

Environmental Consultant

She Tackles Toxic Air in Homes

What Ann Bauman loves most about her job is helping people improve their home environment. "I feel so rewarded when I've helped people get rid of toxins in their home, and they call me and say 'My daughter no longer needs her inhaler,' or 'My son doesn't wake up at night anymore, coughing,' or 'I feel so much better.'"

Ann and her husband, Steve, live in Austin, Texas, and are owners of Millennia Group, a 'green' construction company. Green builders use safe materials that are good for the environment when they build or renovate. They are earth friendly and use natural methods, like catching and using rainwater (harvesting). They use

Environmental Consultant

Consultant fee, visit and basic report, $250

Various tests, $150 to $1,000, depending upon number and type of testing

Income from products, based on percentage of cost

Total income: People who start their own business may not earn any salary in the beginning. They invest their own money in the business, they get more money through loans or venture capital, and, until they make a profit or "go public" by selling stock, they probably pay themselves a small salary and put profits back into the business to help it grow.

wood from trees that grow fast so they don't raid precious forests. They conserve natural landscaping. "Our slogan is 'Creating healthy spaces through consulting, design, construction, remediation [correcting a fault], products, and technology.'"

Ann's buildings don't have the toxic chemicals found in traditional building materials, which is important for everyone, but especially for people who have allergies and immune system illnesses. "Our premise is that if there's one place where you should be able to escape from toxins and challenges to your immune system, it's your home, where you get your rest. You should have as clean an indoor environment as you can get. We're looking at quality of life in a structure where you nurture and take care of yourself.

And, we're also doing something nice for the outside environment."

Mysterious Illness

Around Christmas 1991, Ann thought she had the flu. "I'd stay home, sleep a couple days, then feel okay and return to work. Two days later, I'd fall asleep at my desk." This became a cycle for Ann, but doctors could find nothing wrong. "They told me it was in my mind, or stress, or nerves. They didn't take me seriously. I knew something was wrong."

Ann finally found an immunologist (doctor who studies immune systems) who helped her. She was diagnosed with gradual-onset Chronic Fatigue Immune Dysfunction Syndrome (CFIDS), a virus. "Gradual-onset CFIDS is frustrating. It doesn't hit

Laid off from
sales/computer
systems job

Does integrated
office systems for
Fortune 500 clients

Diagnosed with
multiple chemical
sensitivity

Most people don't know that 82% of
materials used by traditional builders are
known to be toxic, and 26% of those are
known to cause cancer

you all at once. Sometimes I was sick, other times I felt fine. Until I saw this doctor, I began to wonder if it was in my mind. Now I finally knew. I asked him how I could get rid of it. He said 'We don't know.' I was floored."

Later that year, Ann was laid off from her job at Digital Equipment Corporation. "There were general lay-offs, but, in my case, it was an excuse to remove someone who was on dis-ability. I didn't mind, because this is a stress-related illness. So, the pressure of worrying about whether I could work again was making me sicker."

Ann spent the next three years ex-ploring different medicines and treat-ments—holistic, herbal, diet, vitamins. In 1995, she became very ill and was hospitalized. "They told me I had MS (multiple sclerosis—a disease of the central nervous system). I said, 'Oh, I've got MS instead of CFIDS.' They said 'No, you've got both.'"

New Condo Makes Her Sick

Ann moved to Wilmington, North Carolina, to be near her parents. When two back-to-back hurricanes destroyed where she was living, Ann moved into a new condo her parents had bought for rental property. "Within 15 minutes of entering the condo, I was so sick, I had to leave."

Ann then learned she has multiple chemical sensitivity. "My immune system had started breaking down, and it just kept going."

To try to make the condo livable for herself, Ann contacted a green builder (recommended by a friend) who knew all about environmental toxins. "I met Steve and he told me I had unknowingly exposed my already damaged immune system to too many toxins in the new condo." Steve gave Ann lots of books to read, and she started learning about environmental health. "If you have an allergy, it's the first sign that your immune system has had enough, the first sign that your immune system isn't capable of taking care of itself anymore."

Ann learned that different kinds of plants absorb different kinds of toxins, so she identified the toxins in the new condo. "Most people don't know that 82 percent of materials used by traditional builders are known to be toxic, and 26 percent of those are are known to cause cancer." Ann put plants that would absorb these toxins in her condo. "Some plants died from exposure to the toxins." To help the plants remove the toxins and make the condo healthy, Ann bought an ionizing air cleaner. "It was the only thing available at that time. It wasn't a reliable technology, but it helped." After one month, Ann could stay in the condo for a while. After three months, she could spend the night and move in.

All's Well

Ann discussed with Steve her success in making the condo a healthy place to live and her idea for a business venture. "I told him I'd found a way to help people, like myself, and add a little to my income without overworking." Steve gave her some guidance. Ann started talking to CFIDS groups about what she'd learned. "Most CFIDS patients will try anything. I

CAREER CHECKLIST ✓

You'll like this job if you ...

- Are open-minded and flexible
- Are adventuresome
- Are compassionate
- Want to help people
- Like to learn and experiment
- Like to solve problems
- Are comfortable talking to people you don't know and with selling a product

had lots of clients, but they didn't have much money because we're all living on disability or our savings. But this was a great job for me, because I could do most of the work by telephone and send them information." Ann's business grew to include doctors and realtors.

When Steve's business wasn't finding clients, Ann encouraged him to try Austin, Texas. "Wilmington is not an environmentally conscious area, but Austin is very green." So Steve moved to Austin, got some jobs, and asked Ann to join him. "I said 'Sure!'"

Ann moved and set up her business at the beginning of cedar season, a big allergy season in Austin. Steve had found a machine that cleaned the air better than anything they'd used before. "I had an arsenal of information, filters, water purifiers, this machine, and Steve, who has a background in environmental science." Ann put out fliers about her business, called All's Well. "I sold 20 air-cleaning machines in one month, without leaving my apartment." When Steve consulted with people about renovating their houses to make them nontoxic, he referred them to Ann for indoor air quality. "Our businesses started to merge. Eventually, my business joined his— Millennia Group." Ann and Steve also merged into marriage.

Educating People About Green

Millennia Group recently did what many thought impossible. On a lot everyone considered unbuildable, they completed construction of the Villas at Mia Tia Circle, partnered with the city of Austin's Green Builders Program. "The lot we built these four green homes on is hilly, wooded, and was vacant a long time. It's zoned multifamily, for a specified number of units where people can live. A regular builder would have removed all the trees, flattened the lot, and built a high-rise apartment building. We looked at the lot and said 'It's buildable, and we can keep 85 percent of the trees.'"

Ann wanted to use natural methods to make the houses environmentally friendly. "If you're not using city water because you can capture natural rainwater through rainwater harvesting, clean it, and reuse it, that's smart. It's stewardship of the environment by making the best use of what you've got."

fed by the rainwater harvest systems. These waterfalls aerate and clean the air naturally through ionization and provide humidity and healthy 'white' noise that covers traffic noise. One of the houses will get its drinking water from here, so it won't have water bills."

If there's one place where you should be able to escape from toxins and challenges to your immune system, it's your home.

The partnership is using the Villas to educate people about green. "We want to show people these are normal houses, beautiful inside, and we can have clean water and air without expensive filtering systems. We are demonstrating what we can do while being economical and kind to the environment."

When Millennia Group built these houses, they kept 85 percent of the trees and didn't disturb the hill. "We built three houses on top, and one's nestled into the rocks at the bottom. We have three waterfall pools that are

The inside of these houses is just as pretty as the outside and environmentally clean. "We use nontoxic padding for any carpet and recommend nontoxic carpet. We also recommend that everyone leave their shoes, with the dirt, outside. We don't use particle board, we use natural materials that don't outgas (give off toxins). We put bamboo floors in one of the houses; they're gorgeous!" Ann's company used inexpensive ways to exchange stale, indoor air for fresh, outdoor air and get natural lighting.

Members of the partnership plan to show two of the houses for six months. "This isn't a normal showing, where you just wander through the house. We plan to have guides giving tours to explain the materials, how the natural systems work, why this is a good idea, the cost, and the savings over time. These houses look like normal model homes, but they're not." Ann and the partnership plan to make a video of the home tour. They are working on creating a Web site so people can take a virtual tour of these homes when they are no longer open to the public.

Mentor Helps Marketing Career

When Ann was a girl, young girls were expected to grow up and get married rather than have a career. She lived in Milwaukee, Wisconsin, until she was 14 years old and moved to St. Louis, Missouri, where she graduated high school. "I didn't have any career aspirations until high school. It was the mid-1970s when women were starting to break away from traditional roles."

Ann majored in business at South West Texas State College in Missouri. "I had my own personal revolution. When I left college with an associate's degree, the best job I could get was secretarial. I even went to secretarial school after college to get a secretarial degree so I could start at a higher level. But I had no doubt in my mind that I was going to work my way up into the levels of male-dominated businesses without any problems. I was naive."

Ann was a lawyer's secretary for six months, then she took a word-processing job at AMAX Lead and Zinc. "Word processing was becoming very important for companies to record and retrieve data. There were few people who could do it." This skill got her a job at Anheuser-Busch in St. Louis. "Women didn't get above secretary there. But I worked for a marketing executive who recognized my abilities and groomed me for a position he created—market research specialist."

After three years, when she could go no higher in job duties and pay, Ann got a job at Datapoint at the recommendation of her mentor/boss. "He and I worked together to get me into Datapoint at a pretty high level. Women still weren't very accepted in responsible roles. He went to bat for me." With her advanced computer skills, Ann got a job in market support working as a link between the sales and computer systems people. "I was laid off in 1985. It was devastating. I'd broken into the male ranks and was happy with where I was. This was the first time I'd ever lost a job."

Ann got another job in three months. "I told a head hunter I wanted to work in San Antonio or Austin. I gave him three company names; one of them was Digital Equipment Corporation. I got a job as market support analyst with Digital in San Antonio. I felt like everything happened for a reason, because I loved my new job."

Ann progressed up the ranks. In 1989, a group from the corporate office offered her a job in integrated office systems. She moved to Dallas and worked for Digital clients in neighboring states and New England. "I worked with Fortune 500 company executives, helping them make decisions that affected their world-wide corporations."

Ann was doing this work in 1991 when her health began to suffer from CFIDS.

The Perfect Job for Ann

Totally committed to her current work on a clean, green indoor (and outdoor) environment, Ann believes she has the perfect job. "I still have a disabled role. I have to be able to have bad days when I can't work. So, this is the perfect job for someone who wants to set their own hours, work at their own pace, help people's health, and get paid for it."

When she's not working, Ann enjoys reading, genealogy, and writing children's books.

Susan Houghton

Susan Houghton

Farm Manager, Giving Tree Farm, Lansing, MI

Organic, Pesticide-Free Farming

Farm Manager

Earth-Friendly Farmer

Wednesday is Susan Houghton's day off. Every other day finds her at Giving Tree Farm at 7:30 a.m., before anyone else gets there. After Susan has turned the switch that removes the night cover from the greenhouse, she turns on the water to water the plants. Then she determines what must be done that day. "I have a task list that I prepare the day before. But, if something unexpectedly grew a great deal during the night, or the weather got too cold, or the sunshine is making the greenhouse too hot, I deal with those critical situations first. I have to be flexible."

Giving Tree Farm is a 22-acre, certified organic farm in Lansing, Michigan, and Susan is farm manager. "It's a nonprofit organization that was

Farm Manager
Salary ranges from $20,000 to $35,000 a year

SUSAN'S CAREER PATH

Wants to be
▼ farmer

Plays violin, takes
▼ music in college

♫

Marries, has five
▼ children

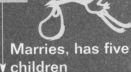

started in 1991 by Carolyn and Robert Bower. They have a medically challenged child, who was two years old when they donated the property for Giving Tree Farm. Giving Tree's mission is to provide disabled persons, their families, and the community with a place to raise organic vegetables and have a good time. It was started as a support group for families with disabled children."

Healthy Plants Make Healthy People

Organic farming means growing plants and raising animals without using synthetic chemicals. For example, farm animals are not given foods that contain hormones to make them grow faster. Plants that give us fruits and vegetables are grown in healthy soil without using synthetic chemical fertilizers. Natural methods, rather than chemical pesticides, are used to get rid of bugs and other pests.

"We can spray water on the plants to blow the bugs off them. If we know we're going to have a pest problem, we can do a preventive garlic spray on the plants. When we have lots of cloudy weather and there is a lot of moisture, we sometimes have a problem with aphids because they like moisture. Then, we treat the plants with an insecticide made from mild soap to get rid of the aphids."

Susan explains, "When a woman is pregnant, she eats healthy foods to produce a healthy baby. Feeding a plant's roots with healthy soil produces a healthy plant and plant product. The high quality of our potting soil gives us a healthy plant. We have

Learns to grow
all food for family

Gets associate degree,
takes accounting job,
divorces

Takes factory job,
meets and marries
Raymond

I want to create an environment that

is socially just, environmentally conscious,

and economically viable.

very few pest problems when we have a healthy plant, because it can naturally defend itself."

Susan's plants are also free of disease. "I haven't seen a disease problem for the plants that I've cared for in years. I'm sure it has to do with quality care. This involves mulching, spreading hay around the plant so that water doesn't splash from the soil to the plant, and a steady supply of moisture and air to the soil so the microbes in the soil can work. They can't live without water and oxygen. If I've created the right environment for the soil, I've also created the right chemical balance to allow the life in the soil do what it's intended to do."

"What I love about my work is the sense of independence. I can provide for myself and my community and provide us with the best food grown anywhere."

Giving Tree Gives to Everyone

"Giving Tree has three programs. The Leisure Garden is a recreational garden. Residents of area group homes

SUSAN'S CAREER PATH

Becomes organic farmer, joins farm organizations

Works with MSU, becomes farm manager

come to grow their own organic vegetables. Our second program provides for a horticultural therapist to train disabled persons in organic farming. (Horticulture is the science of growing fruits, vegetables, flowers, and ornamental plants.) Giving Tree has a state-of-the-art greenhouse with all the environmental controls one could ask for. We train members of this program there. Then we help them find jobs in the horticulture community. The third program is a community-supported agriculture project. We sell shares in the farm's production. This year, we will grow organic vegetables on five acres of certified ground. Some of what we produce will be for the shareholders, and some we will sell at market (at what is called a market garden). The money from the sales helps to pay the farm's expenses. But

our main goal is to support the employment training program."

"Giving Tree is also about building community. The shareholders can come and get their share of the organic vegetables once a week, but many also work 40 hours over the summer to help produce that food. So, our mission includes making the community aware of the environmental, social, and economic issues of organic farming. Everything I've done, till now, has helped me to bring this project full circle."

Down on the Farm, 12 Hours a Day

After she determines what critical issues must be taken care of, Susan helps set up work stations for trainees in the employment training program, which is from 9:30 a.m. to 1:30 p.m.

"Cathy Leavey supervises the training program. Right now we're teaching seeding and transplanting." Susan even works through lunch. "The horticultural therapist and I have lunch together and talk about what we'll do in the afternoon. After lunch, I set up for the next day—prepare the task list by deciding what we are going to do and who is going to do it." Giving Tree has 50 volunteers, and Susan is teaching them how to transplant. "I show them what good roots look like, and I talk about what kind of insect problems we're having and what plant variety we are planting. A big part of my job is education." At the end of her 12-hour day, Susan closes the greenhouse cover to retain the heat from the day's sunshine and locks the doors.

Hoop Houses and Other Innovations

Susan also works in organic agriculture and its promotion with Michigan State University (MSU), which is located in East Lansing, not far from her

CAREER CHECKLIST ✓

You'll like this job if you ...

- Like the outdoors
- Like to get your hands in the dirt
- Are determined and patient
- Are independent and a risk-taker
- Like to solve problems
- Like to read, observe, and learn on your own
- Can sort out what's important from lots of information

home in Lansing. "I've developed my own mixture of potting soil which they are interested in. I'm also working with a horticultural specialist at MSU to study what crops can be grown in unheated hoop houses (a framework structure covered with plastic). Over the years, I've built two hoop houses, each 12 feet wide and 75 feet long, to extend our growing season, because Michigan's summers are so short. I learned that I can grow lettuce and other greens all year, even with Michigan's long winters and cloudy weather. This means I can provide fresh vegetables in winter, instead of ones shipped here from California. Shipped vegetables lose vitamins and minerals because they sit for so long." Susan also helps university researchers with grant coordination.

Tells Mom She Wants to be a Farmer

Susan was born in Akron, Ohio. Her father served in the U.S. military. When she was four years old, her parents moved to North Canton, Ohio. "When I was very young, I visited my grandparents, who lived in Buffalo, Ohio, about 100 miles away. My grandfather had a beautiful garden, and I helped my grandmother can green beans. She gave my mother lots of her canned food. While growing up, I had memories of my grandmother's canned food and the great flavor. Later in life, when I had to buy food for my family, the store-bought canned food never tasted as good as my grandmother's."

When she was 16 years old, Susan told her mother that she wanted to be a farmer. "I told her that I loved having my hands in the dirt and that I wanted to pursue some sort of farming studies." Susan's mother was not quite receptive to her daughter becoming a farmer. "She told me that I was better than that. Her family had been farmers, so she knew how farmers had to struggle to make a good living or pursue what many think is a good life."

In high school, Susan studied college prep courses and played violin, which she began when she was nine

GROUNDBREAKERS
The Mother of Balboa Park

In 1892, Katherine Olivia Sessions (1857-1940) leased land for a nursery in what was called San Diego, California's City Park. For this privilege, she was to plant 100 trees a year in the park and furnish 300 more for planting throughout the city. In 1902 she and friends George Marston and Mary B. Coulston formed the Park Improvement Committee, which assured the park's place in the life of the community.

Sessions began her horticultural career after teaching briefly in San Diego, where she had accepted a position in 1884 after graduating from the University of California at Berkeley. She joined her friends, Mr. And Mrs. Solon Blaisdell, as a partner in the purchase of the San Diego Nursery.

Sessions became a central figure in California and national horticultural circles with her landscaping, plant introductions, and classes. She owned a flower shop and a succession of nurseries in Coronado, City Park, Mission Hills, and Pacific Beach. She helped found the San Diego Floral Association and was appointed supervisor of agriculture and landscaper for San Diego city schools in 1915.

Sessions's correspondence with leaders in the field kept her current. Her work in plant introduction won international recognition for her and, in 1939, she was awarded the prestigious Frank N. Meyer Medal of the American Genetic Association, the first woman to receive the award. The Tipuana tipu tree planted by Sessions still stands on the former site of her nursery at Garnet and Pico in Pacific Beach. It is now a California Registered Historical Landmark.

Source: San Diego Historical Society, Web site: www.sandiego history.org

years old. "I was a concert mistress in high school." She attended Cottey College in Nevada, Missouri, where she continued playing violin and pursued music. "I played in a quartet in college. But I struggled with it. I knew that I was never going to write music or be a professional musician." She left college after one year and worked in a tax office.

Grows Food to Feed Family

When Susan's grandfather died, her grandmother moved to St. Petersburg, Florida. When her grandmother became ill, Susan moved there to care for her. She met and married her first husband in Florida, and after her grandmother died, Susan and her husband moved to Cadillac, Michigan. They had five children. "We lived on a farm; I was not going to live in town. My contribution to the family's income was to grow food for the family. I learned how to grow strawberries, tomatoes, peaches, everything—I learned how to grow all our food. But with five kids, buying fertilizers and pesticides was outside our budget. So, I learned how to improve the quality of the soil and provide healthy food by reading books about growing organic gardens. I also learned to observe what was going on in my own garden. I came to learn that the biggest part of growing organically is learning about what goes on in my own space."

Susan and her family moved to White Pigeon, Michigan, where she had a half acre of land on which to grow vegetables. When her youngest child was 13 years old, "I decided I needed to know more and be a little more independent, so I went to Glen Oaks Community College in Centreville, Michigan. I earned an associate degree in business and data processing. Then I found an accounting job." When Susan and her husband divorced, she still had three teenage children to support, and the office job didn't pay enough, so she took a higher paying job in a factory. "I did that job for five years." During this time, Susan met Raymond Houghton.

Becomes an Organic Farmer

After she married Raymond, Susan was able to quit her factory job and return to farming. "By this time, I was sure I wanted to be an organic farmer. The National Organic Production Act had passed into law, and I searched for an organization to help me understand what the law meant and how it would apply to a market garden." Susan found an organic growers organization in Michigan and volunteered to edit their newsletter. "It's a good way to get acquainted and learn."

Then, Susan and her family moved to Bristol, Indiana, where they bought a four-acre farm, and Susan started a market garden. "With my father's help, I designed and built a greenhouse. I wanted it to be as energy efficient as possible, so we built it to use geothermal heat. We put water hoses in the ground. The water circulates through them and then through solar water heaters. From there, it goes into a 400-gallon water tank. The heat storage is contained inside the greenhouse." Susan learned a lot about herself from this project. "I learned that I have a lot of imagination for problem-solving, which is necessary for organic farming. You also need a different way of looking at equipment. Traditional farm equipment doesn't apply to organic farming."

Susan worked as produce manager for the Centre-In Co-op where she learned how to handle produce. As she learned more about organic procedures, she became chairperson of the southwest chapter of Organic Growers of Michigan. She went on to become chairperson of the state level organization and is now the state level vice-chairperson.

In 1997, Susan brought independent organic inspectors to Michigan for training. She took the course herself and was certified to be an organic inspector. She conducted 200 inspections for the Organic Crop Improvement Association and Organic Growers of Michigan from Iowa to Ohio, and she worked on some dairy farms in Wisconsin.

Stephanie Shakofsky

Stephanie Shakofsky

Executive Director, California Center for Land Recycling, San Francisco, CA

Major in Geology; master's degree in Hydrogeology, San Jose State University, CA

Toxic Clean-Up—Restoration of Brownfields

Executive Director

Bringing Abandoned Communities to Life

"We are rapidly gobbling up our forests and natural habitats and threatening the life of this planet. This dire fact has led me to find workable solutions to the problems of housing and feeding people while assuring good habitats exist for all other living creatures." This mission has led Stephanie Shakofsky to her work in redeveloping and recycling contaminated land in urban areas, helping communities make them useful again.

Stephanie is executive director of the California Center for Land Recycling (CCLR) in San Francisco. "What I like best about this job is that it marries my education, my skills, and

Executive, nonprofit organization
Salary range from $25,000 to $350,000 a year, depending on organization, its size, and location

my life's experience with CCLR's mission—to help communities reclaim the abandoned or contaminated areas in their communities." Stephanie has learned about contaminated soil and ground water and seen the social and environmental implications of loss of habitat and continuous sprawl, when green spaces surrounding cities are devel-

oped into housing, shopping centers, and industrial areas.

Because CCLR is a nonprofit organization, it relies on donations from foundations, individuals, and corporations for the money it needs to fulfill its mission. "I spend a lot of time talking to people about CCLR's mission and goals to get funding." And she manages the staff, works on budgets, and directs the work projects.

Helping Where It's Needed

"We work with the citizens of struggling and distressed communities, where abandoned properties and contaminated sites exist." For example, CCLR is working with Habitat for

Works at USGS,
researches toxins in soil
and ground water

Marries Mike,
takes job analyzing
proposed laws

Moves to
Connecticut,
works on pollution

Humanity (a foundation started by former president Jimmy Carter to restore old or build new homes for lower-income people). The group plans to buy an abandoned gas station property in a residential neighborhood and build three homes. "We review proposals and help the project's supporters work through the legal and regulatory maze. One reason people don't redevelop these lands is the cost to clean up the contamination. But the legal and regulatory processes also scare people from redeveloping older, abandoned sites and drive them to develop green sites, instead. Our project support removes some of the costs and gets people through the nightmarish processes."

Stephanie's staff members also write policy papers. They try to influence debates and get laws changed to make it harder to develop green spaces and easier to redevelop abandoned land areas. "Right now, the scales are totally tipped against redevelopment." Stephanie works 12-hour days, from 7 a.m. to 7 p.m., Monday through Friday, and she often works weekends. Her office is four blocks from her home because "I made a decision to walk to work." She wears suits for meetings with foundation representatives but dresses casually other times. Although her project managers do more site visits, Stephanie does travel for her job because CCLR is a state-wide organization.

"It is very rewarding to work with people who want to revitalize their community and to help keep people and businesses in the older urban areas instead of sprawling over green spaces. It's exciting to see these projects succeed."

77

Saving Frogs Inspires Her

Stephanie's inspiration to work in urban land recycling came when she was executive director of the Soil and Water Conservation District in eastern Connecticut. One of the responsibilities of her job was to map vernal pools. "Vernal pools are small bodies of water that occur when spring rains fill shallow depressions in the forest landscape. Amphibians, like salamanders and frogs, who live most of the year in the woods, have evolved to deposit their eggs only in vernal pools, largely because there are no fish in these pools, and fish are the largest predators of amphibian eggs. When the frogs and salamanders are old enough, they leave the pools and live in the woods. In spring, they instinctively return to the same pool they came from to breed and deposit their eggs, even if their pool has been paved over. This is what's happening when a lot of frogs turn up in a new store's parking lot. The new store has wiped out their breeding ground, and so that population will die out. We're wiping out amphibian populations worldwide."

Stephanie's group mapped these vernal pools so the municipalities and property owners know about them. "We've learned that vernal pools have a relationship to healthy forests, and they exist for a very short period of time in the spring. So they are easily overlooked and get plowed under for new development."

The city leaders planned to build an industrial park in a forested, undeveloped area near town, that was covered with vernal pools. "Yet, they had miles of abandoned industrial sites along the waterfront. Since frogs can't vote, it was much easier and cheaper to build on this green site. This was a barbaric proposal and shows just what a throw-away society we are. People say, 'We've used this land; it's polluted; it'll cost too much to clean it up, so let's abandon it. We can build over there.' That's when I became more involved, actively educating the community about the vernal pools."

Teacher Sparks Imagination

Stephanie grew up in Glendale, Missouri, the eighth of ten children. "No one in my family went to college, so I thought I'd be a typist, like my mother, or a secretary or waitress like my older sisters." Stephanie liked school, but says she wasn't a great student. She did have some good teachers who inspired her. "One fourth grade teacher loved science. She sparked everyone's imagination with her curiosity, imagination, and

CAREER CHECKLIST ✓

You'll like this job if you ...

Like nature and the outdoors

Are assertive and competitive

Are well read and well rounded

Know and understand science well

Understand the social implications of environmental policies

Like to work with all kinds of people

Can communicate well

quest for discovery." Girl Scouts also influenced Stephanie. "Their emphasis on community service and appreciation of nature has stayed with me."

Stephanie decided she wanted to go to college and attended the University of Illinois in Champaign-Urbana. "I knew that I didn't want to be a typist, and I needed a college education, but I didn't know I was going to be a scientist. It was during college that I realized my love of science, especially geology. The field trips were an added attraction—I liked being outdoors."

Stephanie had no family role models nor money for college. "I was a pioneer in my family; it was difficult." She applied for grants, scholarships, and loans and worked to pay for college. "I struggled for money, and I chose a male-dominated field. There were three or four women in a class of 30. It wasn't just the male classmates. It was especially difficult with the older male professors." But Stephanie succeeded because she loved to study and loved science. "When someone told me I couldn't do something, it just reinforced me,

challenged me to do it." Growing up with two older brothers helped give Stephanie the experience she needed to take care of herself and compete in a male-dominated profession.

Studies to be a Wet Geologist

"My first love is paleontology (study of fossils), but to be a paleontologist, you really need a Ph.D. from a college like Yale, and there is a lot of competition for a few great jobs. So, I had to think really hard about my graduate studies. I remember one of my professors telling me, 'If you get wet in geology, you'll always be employed.' This meant the study of water and its interactions with rock. There will always be interest in water."

After graduating college, Stephanie did salvage archeology in the Mississippi Valley. "In the survey, we searched for artifacts, dug them up, and documented them, one step in front of the bulldozer. It was fun, but it was hard, physical work that was seasonal and didn't pay much."

After one year, Stephanie moved to California to attend graduate school at San Jose State University. "Having grown up and lived in the Midwest all my life, California was exotic to me." She again got grants and loans to pay for a master's degree in hydrogeology. "My major thesis professor, June Oberdorfer, was my first role model. I learned about June when I was looking into which graduate school I would attend. I chose to study with her because she was a renowned hydrologist and a woman. June helped me get a job in the water resources section of the United States Geological Survey (USGS), a federal agency devoted to research in geological science. So, I went to school part time and worked at USGS part time, where I had the opportunity to do science and my master's thesis and get paid all at the same time."

Learns about Contaminants

After two years, Stephanie earned her master's degree and began working

GROUNDBREAKERS
Hazards of Nuclear Energy

Karen Gay Silkwood's (1946-1974) life and death emphasized the hazards of nuclear energy and raised questions about corporate responsibility. In 1972, Silkwood took a job as a metallography laboratory technician at the Cimarron River plutonium plant of Kerr-McGee Nuclear Corporation in Crescent, Oklahoma. She joined the Oil, Chemical, and Atomic Workers Union.

In 1974, she became the first female member of the union bargaining committee in Kerr-McGee history. On her first assignment to study health and safety issues at the plant, she discovered evidence of spills, leaks, and missing plutonium. From November 5 until her death November 13, 1974, Silkwood was involved in a number of unexplained exposures to plutonium. Her apartment was surveyed and significant levels of activity were found—high levels in the bathroom and kitchen, and lower levels in other rooms. She was killed in a one-car crash while on her way to meet with an Atomic Energy Commission official and a *New York Times* newspaper reporter.

Speculations over foul play in her death were never substantiated, but led to a federal investigation into plant security and safety, and a National Public Radio report about 44 to 66 pounds of misplaced plutonium. Kerr-McGee closed the plant in 1975. In 1984, Silkwood was the subject of a motion picture, *Silkwood*.

Source: *The Handbook of Texas Online*, a joint project of the General Libraries at the University of Texas at Austin and the Texas State Historical Association. 1998 PBS and WGBH/"Frontline."

full time as a research hydrologist at USGS. "We studied the processes and mechanisms that determine how fast contaminants (pollution) move through the soil and ground water (contaminant transport). It varies for different contaminants and different geological environments."

Stephanie's research included working at a nuclear-designated federal facility in Idaho and at Yucca Mountain, Nevada, where the federal government is trying to establish a repository (underground vault) in which they can store nuclear (radioactive) waste. "Radioactive contaminants tend to cling to the soil and not move too far. So, this soil can be removed and stored in a safer place. It would be smart to have a repository, but nobody wants one in their state."

"I was a good scientist, but there's something very secluded about scientific research. You're alone or with one or two people in the lab or field. One part of me really thrived in that environment, but the other part of me was much more people and community oriented. I was more interested in the social implications of contamination."

Lawsuit Leads to Marriage

Stephanie was active in environmental issues in her community. A group she was working with was opposed to a planned development along the San Francisco Bay. "I worked with them to file a lawsuit against the city. The mayor of the city—his name was Mike—was the spokesperson for the city. He really impressed me. He was very concerned about the natural environment, a lover of wildlife and hiking, and committed to social change. So, we were able to negotiate a settlement." Stephanie and Mike later 'negotiated' a marriage.

Technical Analyst for California Legislature

When an opportunity to become a technical analyst for the California state legislature arose, Stephanie seized the moment. The job was analyst for the

Toxic Environmental Safety Committee. "This is a powerful policy committee. All proposed bills and regulations affecting the environment and toxic cleanup must pass through the committee. My job was to analyze whether it was a good bill or a bad bill." So, after six years at USGS, Stephanie moved to Sacramento to become a committee advisor who analyzed California's proposed environmental and toxic laws.

After Stephanie worked one year for the California legislature, Mike decided to go to law school. He was accepted at Yale. "We talked about whether I should stay in California to continue my work while he moved to Connecticut, or whether I could find meaningful work there and move with him. We were newly married and wanted to stay together, so I started hunting for environmental jobs in Connecticut. I found an ad on a website for environmental jobs. I interviewed and got the job." This job was executive director of the Soil and Water Conservation District in eastern Connecticut.

Stephanie loved her job. "The Soil and Water Conservation districts were established at President Franklin D. Roosevelt's request during the worst ecological disaster this nation has ever experienced—the Dust Bowl. President Roosevelt realized that conservation education was sorely needed and that education had to happen at the local level. He urged every state to establish local conservation districts."

Back to California

Then one day Stephanie got a call from California. "I knew about CCLR. I had talked to the executive director about redevelopment when I worked for California's legislature. When he decided to leave CCLR, he called me to ask if I was interested in his job. I said, 'Give me five seconds to think about it.'" Mike was in his last year of law school. He and Stephanie knew they wanted to return to California, so she took the job.

When she's not working at CCLR, Stephanie loves to hike and canoe. She's still very involved in her community and enjoys educating people about her work.

Donna Leonard

Donna Leonard

Entomologist, Forest Health Protection Division, State and Private Forestry, U.S. Department of Agriculture Forest Service, Asheville, NC

Major in Forestry; master's degree in Forestry with Entomology concentration, Clemson University, SC

Forest Health Protection Entomologist

It's War Against a Small But Powerful Pest

Gypsy moths were brought to Massachusetts in the mid 1800s for the purpose of breeding with silkworms to produce a hardy strain of silkworms that could survive in the northeastern United States. But it didn't work (different species cannot breed and produce offspring). The moths escaped, became established, and have been spreading south and westward ever since. By early 2001, the entire Northeast had been generally infested with the gypsy moth, as had portions of Virginia, West Virginia, Ohio, Indiana, Illinois, Wisconsin, and Michigan. When the moths go into what is called outbreak, thousands, even millions of the small, hairy caterpillars (that turn into gypsy moths) can swarm over trees,

U.S. Forest Service, State and Private Division

GS 7 to GS 13 (depending upon experience and years of service), $30,000 to $75,000 per year
GS 15 (with doctoral degree), $110,000 per year

homes, and patios. Donna Leonard's job is to slow the spread of these pests that destroy the leaves of trees and plants and greatly annoy people.

Donna is an entomologist (a person who studies insects). She works for the U.S. Forest Service in the Forest Health Protection Division. She is in charge of a program called Slow the Spread (STS), and she works with people in the nine states that include the

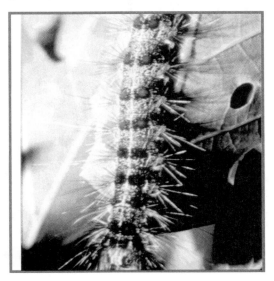

expanding front of the gypsy moth population. "We work in a borderline area 1,200 miles long and 65 miles wide, starting in Michigan's Upper Peninsula, through Wisconsin, Illinois, Indiana, Ohio, Kentucky, West Virginia, Virginia, and North Carolina."

Gypsy moths are an exotic species to the United States because they did not evolve here. They are native to Europe and parts of Asia where they are kept in check by a complex of natural enemies. Unfortunately, many of these natural enemies do not live in the United States.

"In the years that the government has been involved with the gypsy moth problem," Donna says, "they have gone back to the native range and collected the moth's natural enemies and released them here. Some of these biological controls have helped.

But there is always a risk in releasing another exotic, because they can upset the natural balance and threaten native species."

Researchers have a selection of ways to manage the gypsy moth, one of which is the application of insecticides by spraying from the air (aerial). Most of these insecticides used to battle gypsy moth outbreaks can kill caterpillars of other moths and butterflies. This can indirectly affect birds and bats by reducing their food supply.

The Slow the Spread program is using a new method. "I am really excited about what we're doing now, which is called mating disruption. It targets only the gypsy moth, so it doesn't harm any other critters, including other moths and butterflies. Researchers have been able to isolate, identify, and synthesize (duplicate)

the gypsy moth pheromone, which is a chemical emitted by the female moth. Adult females cannot fly to find their mates, so they use the pheromone to attract the males to them when they are ready to mate. We use the synthetic pheromone for both survey and control. It can be used as a bait in sticky traps so we can monitor gypsy moth populations. It can be loaded into controlled-release dispensers and used as a treatment to control the small infestations in the STS area by confusing the males so they cannot find the females to mate."

Out in the STS Zone

Workers in the various states lay some 90,000 pheromone-baited, sticky traps in a grid pattern before the gypsy

Earned master's degree in Forestry/Entomology

Put in charge of Slow the Spread program

In a male-dominated profession like forestry, many men were suspicious of me and felt women weren't meant to be working in this field.

moths begin to fly. Then at the end of August, the traps are collected and the findings are entered into a computer database for analysis. Plans for the next year's treatment projects are based on the analysis. "We typically find infestations on about 200,000 acres per year, and most of these are treated using mating disruption."

Donna's job takes her out of the office beginning in mid-April, as she travels to visit the different states where the treatment sites are located. "As the leaves come out, the caterpillars come

out. A big part of my job is to provide technical assistance to the folks at the various state agencies who do most of the work. Technology for safe and effective aerial spray programs is continually advancing, and there is always a need to train new people. When we use airplanes to spray, we used to put a lot of people in the field to mark the corners of each specific spray area with helium-filled balloons so the pilots could be sure they were treating the proper area. But now we use the GPS (geographic positioning system via satellite) and computers, which have streamlined and improved the entire process. We still have a few people out in the treatment block, because we need to monitor the weather and other important factors."

Job Changes with the Seasons

Donna's job has a lot of variety. In the office in early spring on a typical day, Donna may be working on several things. Perhaps she's preparing a slide presentation she will give about the program, usually about the science behind the STS project. She may be analyzing the potential impact of a proposed treatment on soil, water, and endangered species. (This analysis is required by law. If the impact is too 'significant,' the proposed treatment will not go forward.) And she may be working out the details of a contract with a pilot who will actually do the aerial spraying. She spends lots of time coordinating the timing and details of the projects, which can start as early as mid-April in coastal North Carolina

CAREER CHECKLIST ✓

You'll like this job if you ...

- Like working outside

- Don't mind getting dirty

- Think bugs like ants, spiders, moths, and beetles are interesting

- Are curious about bug behavior

- Find science interesting

and go through the end of June in the northern part of Wisconsin.

From mid-April to mid-July, Donna will be traveling to help out at the various treatment projects where technical support might be needed and to see how things are going. During July and August, she is back in the office getting her neglected paperwork done.

In the fall, the data starts coming in and is analyzed. Then meetings with each state group begin. Donna goes over the data with the local officials, and together they plan the 'attack' for next spring. These meetings finish up by late November. The wintertime is spent preparing for next spring.

"I love this work, being in on refining the mating disruption program, improving it. I'm involved in testing new systems and designing new protocols and guidelines for use in the STS project. And I like talking with people about the STS program. I'm a people person, and I enjoy the teamwork we have with the state and federal agency people. Scientists often disagree, so there may be conflict involved. We all have our own points of view, which we express. But I enjoy the process. Some of the best ideas come when we work out these conflicts, and this builds a better program."

"My division also has a responsibility to take new research from the U.S. Forest Service research folks and put it into practice. That part is really challenging."

Chooses to Study Forestry

Donna saw quite a bit of the world growing up in a military family—Germany, Russia, France, and several states. "I had lots of extra activities like piano lessons, languages, even ballroom dancing. I didn't think much about what I'd do when I grew up, but I enjoyed school, and it seemed natural to go to college."

At the University of the South, in Sewanee, Tennessee, Donna discovered forestry. "It was a small campus on a large land area that offered hiking, caves, waterfalls, and lots of woods. I loved being outdoors and really enjoyed the forestry labs, which were held outdoors." When she graduated, Donna 'fell into' a summer job in the Cherokee National Forest in the mountains of eastern Tennessee. It was 1976, and she was hired as a teacher for a youth conservation corps program. She and her crew of teenagers did things like building and maintaining trails, patrolling campgrounds, and studying environmental science.

When summer ended, Donna found a job with a timber company in Georgia. The first woman to be hired there, she got experience in many types of work. She worked in land acquisition, covering 18 counties, with land varying from thick vegetation to swamp

GROUNDBREAKERS
Under-the-Sea Pioneer

On October 7, 2000, Sylvia Earle—acclaimed marine biologist, author, and cofounder of a company that builds deep-sea submersibles—was inducted into the National Women's Hall of Fame.

Earle (born 1935) loves the ocean, and when a child was fascinated with horseshoe crabs, starfish, and tiny seaweed creatures. She enjoys descending hundreds of feet, bringing her, she says, face-to-face with the "sparkle, flash, and glow" of a shining world that resembles "a galaxy of living stars." Earle was the first to make use of the modern SCUBA gear (self-contained underwater breathing apparatus). In her more than 6,000 hours underwater, Earle has discovered many new species of marine life and documented marine ecosystems. In 1979, she planted the Stars and Stripes on the ocean floor in history's deepest solo dive without a tether to the surface. She descended to 1,250 feet strapped to the front of a submarine, then stepped off to walk around and make her observations.

Earle co-founded Deep Ocean Engineering in 1981, and in 1984, the company set a world record for solo diving with Earle aboard its Deep Rover. An internationally known champion for ocean conservation, Earle has lectured in more than 50 countries, appeared on television, has written many articles, and serves on boards of directors. She has three children and three grandchildren.

Source: National Women's Hall of Fame, Web site: www.greatwomen.org

(which she had to walk following a straight survey line). Her job was to find out what land was for sale, assessing the value of the timber, and determining what the company should offer to pay for the land. She also learned to work in a bucket truck, being lifted up to the tops of trees. She worked with tree-seedling projects and with tree-improvement projects. Donna often dealt with loggers, making sure they were doing what the company wanted and determining what they would be paid. "In a male-dominated profession, many were suspicious of me, and many felt women were not meant to be working in this field. They didn't appreciate a 22-year-old female telling them what they should be doing."

Back to the Mountains

After two years at the company, Donna decided to move to Asheville, North Carolina, and join her boyfriend Pete, whom she had been dating since they met at her sister's wedding during Donna's senior year of college. They were married that fall.

When looking for a job, Donna discovered that a person whom she had met when attending a conference on tree improvement worked with the Forest Service in Asheville. She called on him, and it turned out that he needed a technician to drive a bucket truck and do tree-top surveys for an orchard tree-improvement project. Donna took the job at the end of that year.

In the mid-1980s, Donna applied for and got an opportunity to enter the Forest Service's long-term training program. She went to Clemson University in South Carolina full time for one semester, taking 22 hours of coursework. "I studied entomology because I liked the idea of pest management to protect our forests. My entomology professor encouraged me to finish my degree, but I decided against further study at that time." Upon completion of the semester, she went into a trainee entomologist position that lasted for a year.

"In 1986, the gypsy moth was just beginning to encroach upon the southern forests. I began working with a lot of experts; many held Ph.D. degrees. I felt uneducated, so I decided to go back and finish my master's degree. I took a leave of absence and went back to Clemson for one semester. Then I returned to work. I was able to incorporate the field work for my thesis into my job—using mating disruption to control populations of insects. I got involved in the development of the technology, and my field work was a controlled test site."

After earning her master's in Forestry with a concentration on Entomology, Donna continued working with Forest Health Protection, where she eventually became the STS program manager.

Donna and Pete own their own home, where Donna loves to work in her flower garden. "I love flowers but I'm just beginning to learn how to grow them. One of the nicest parts of having flowers in your yard is that you also get lots of butterflies and hummingbirds." Donna also loves to read novels, and, despite all the travel she does for work, she and Pete enjoy "traveling for fun."

Sarah Liehr

Sarah Liehr

Research Assistant Professor, Department of Biological and Agricultural Engineering, North Carolina State University, Raleigh, NC

Major, Biology; master's degree in Applied Limnology; Ph.D., Environmental Science in Civil Engineering, University of Illinois, Champaign-Urbana

Waste Management —Farm Animals
Researcher

Animal Waste Clean-Up, Naturally

Sarah Liehr's job lets her do everything she loves. She's a research assistant professor at North Carolina State University, conducting research to find better ways to treat animal waste (manure). Her work involves finding effective and affordable ways for farmers to treat waste.

"I love biology more than anything in the world. I get to work with the natural processes of biology, with chemistry, and with the physical properties of wastewater treatment systems—making these sciences work together to meet treatment goals." Sarah likes problem solving. "I get to use math; that's fun. I do a lot of modeling on the computer and that involves math, describing a treatment system and predicting

Environmental Engineer
Bachelor's degree starting salary, $38,000 to $40,000 a year
Master's degree starting salary, $41,000 and higher a year
Research Assistant Professor
Academic/faculty position starting salary, $50,000 to $65,000 a year

SARAH'S CAREER PATH

Likes performing
arts, chasing
bugs

Graduates college,
earns master's
degree

Works for Natural
History Survey,
marries Ted

Though I liked chasing bugs and

being in water, finding what I wanted to do

has been a wandering process for me.

I didn't focus on one thing.

what it will do. And I like research, solving old problems in new ways."

Protecting the environment is valuable and important to Sarah, who notes, "The environmental impacts may be hidden or not realized immediately when treating waste with high-technology methods (the impact of generating electricity; the production of chemicals and materials used in the processes). That's why I like developing low-impact technologies that use natural environmental systems and work with nature."

Sarah also likes her working relationships. "People are important here—the faculty and staff people I work with, the students, and the people we're trying to help. We all work together to solve problems."

The Animal Waste Problem

"There are more contaminants (especially nutrients, oxygen demand, and suspended solids) in animal wastewater, especially hog waste, than in

Earns Ph.D., teaches
at University of
Houston

Joins NCSU
faculty, has
daughter Amelia

Doesn't get
tenure, leaves
job

city wastewater. So, the technologies for treating city wastewater don't always work as well for animal waste." The low-impact treatment technologies in Sarah's research projects don't require lots of machinery, maintenance, energy, money, and expertise to operate. "Cost is a big issue for farmers. They can't afford to pay for a treatment system that requires expensive, high-maintenance machinery or to hire a treatment expert and still make enough money to survive."

Along with contaminant removal, Sarah's research projects seek better ways to recover the nutrients. "Recovered nitrogen and phosphorus can be used as fertilizer. The challenge is to recover and package them so they become a useful product rather than waste. Currently North Carolina is importing more nutrients through feeding its animals than we can use on our crops. Methane and ethanol (types of energy sources) are also products to recover." Sarah says, "I've worked with other researchers on a methane-recovery project that allows the farmers to produce electricity for their own use on the farm. Right now, the process costs too much for most farmers, but that could change if the cost of other electricity sources goes higher."

Big Farms Equal Big Problems

Animal waste has become a big problem in states like North Carolina and Iowa, where there are many huge farms. "Huge farms have changed the way animals are raised. Technologies developed to treat waste from smaller farms aren't appropriate for the big farms we have now." Sarah notes that "One common older technology uses anaerobic (without oxygen) lagoons (open pits) where waste is flushed from the animal houses with water. The waste remains in the lagoon for a long time while microorganisms, mostly naturally occurring bacteria, break it down into a substance that can be sprayed onto fields as fertilizer."

"For huge farms, there are huge anaerobic lagoons with large surface areas. They can have lots of problems, depending on the size of the lagoon and how much waste you put into it, and how well it is managed." Two main problems are the potential for overflow during heavy rains or floods, which pollutes rivers and lakes, and leaking if bottom linings fail, which may pollute underground water.

"Today, regulations for lagoons require that they have enough extra space to allow for heavy rains. If the lagoon is being operated properly, it should have excess storage space for rainfall. Current design standards are geared to prevent leaking into the groundwater. If it's not a concrete or steel tank, a pond/lagoon must be lined with plastic or clay to prevent leakage into the groundwater. Not all lagoons built before the regulations were implemented are effective at preventing leaks. Our inspection system needs to make sure lagoons are structurally sound and being operated properly."

People complain about another problem with lagoons—the smell. In North Carolina, regulations require that water from lagoons not go into a fresh body of water because lagoon water isn't clean enough. Farmers must apply this water to the land in a way that nutrients in the water can be taken up by the plants, only applying the amount of water that the crop can use. Sarah says, "The problem is also the way it's applied—some farmers spray the water up into the air onto the fields. This causes the water and the odor to spread. Once it's on the ground, it's not as big of a problem."

Finding New Technologies for New Farming

When bacteria break down the organics in the waste, oxygen is consumed. When there is no oxygen in the water,

CAREER CHECKLIST ✓

You'll like this job if you ...

Want to protect the environment

Like biology, math, chemistry

Would enjoy computer modeling

Like to design systems

Want to solve problems

Like to work outdoors

Are analytical

the water smells bad and nothing can live in the water. Anaerobic lagoons allow this to happen in a controlled area, rather than in a body of fresh water. "But," Sarah says, "there are other ways of designing and operating lagoons." Lagoons can have aerators (machines that circulate air/oxygen through the wastewater to help purify it), which helps the bacteria break down the organics faster. "With aerators, what would happen naturally in a stream or lake—using the oxygen—happens in the lagoon."

Another technology is constructed wetlands. "These are not the natural wetlands but are wetlands built specifically for wastewater treatment. They use wetland plants, like cattails and bull rushes, and have a free-water surface, like a marsh. You can vary the water depth to maximize nutrient removal from the wastewater by the bacteria that grow on the plants and in the soil. The key is to make the bacterial population the right one for removing the nutrients and contaminants." Sarah adds, "To make this work, solids suspended in the wastewater must first be removed. This is one hard part of treating hog waste. We're evaluating technologies for that—settling, filtering, and even centrifuges (machines that spin their contents to separate different elements of the contents)."

Sarah notes that a series of lagoons, instead of one big lagoon, is a good technology. "The first lagoon may aerate the dirtiest water; the second lagoon receives the aerated water and may be where the solids settle; then the water may go through more lagoons for additional processes. The wastewater is circulated through the organized series of lagoons, designed to get the most from the bacteria, which remove the contaminants. Some systems being studied add bacteria. The systems I'm studying use natural organisms that are there all the time."

Sarah's Day

Sarah's drive to work takes five minutes; she arrives about 9 a.m. "The time is flexible, so I can get my daughter, Amelia, to school. I work some weekends and can take work home when I have to leave early, before 5:30 p.m." Sarah wears "grungy field clothes" when she must work outdoors, but she dresses up for important meetings. "Most of the time, I'm dressed comfortably."

Most of Sarah's tasks focus on developing strategies and studying economical technologies for treatment of hog waste. She must do lots of paperwork to apply for grants to pay for her research. She applies for grants from federal and state sources and also for private funding from technological companies and food processing companies like Smithfield Foods. Sarah finalizes reports for completed projects, which involves data analysis and writing about conclusions drawn from the research. She works with her students' projects to set up and monitor equipment for evaluating treatment systems on farms. She oversees the design and set-up of laboratory experiments and the development of mathematical models. "One student's model is being developed to predict how efficiently dif-

GROUNDBREAKERS
Perserving Florida's Treasure

Marjorie Stoneman Douglas (1890-1998) was a journalist and author. After World War I, when she served with the American Red Cross in Europe, she launched her career as a newspaper editor at her father's paper, which later became *The Miami Herald*. It was a time of rapid development in southern Florida, and she began writing both fiction and nonfiction about environmental issues.

In 1947, her book *The Everglades: River of Grass* became a bestseller. It raised people's awareness and transformed the Florida Everglades from an area that was looked upon as a useless swamp (to be drained and developed commercially) to a national park to be protected and preserved.

Douglas lived long enough to see Florida voters pass in 1996 a constitutional amendment that held polluters primarily responsible for cleaning up the Everglades. Today, projects are underway to restore the Everglades. Douglas received the Presidential Medal of Freedom in 1993 at age 103.

Source: National Women's Hall of Fame, Web site: www.great women.org

ferent treatment systems work to protect the environment across large regions of North Carolina."

Didn't Know What Career She Wanted

Sarah grew up in Galva, a small town in north-central Illinois. "As a girl, I didn't think about having a serious career. I liked music, drama, art, but I also liked chasing bugs and being in water. I never thought about it as a career." When Sarah was in high school, she realized that she liked biology more than anything else. "I started college as a biology education major. I dropped education after one year. There were too many biology courses I wanted to take." Sarah still didn't know what career she would have with a biology degree.

To help pay for her education at the University of Illinois, Champaign-Urbana, Sarah worked part time as a lab assistant and did computer programming. In her senior year, she took a course in limnology, the study of fresh-water bodies, like lakes. "I just loved it. I thought, 'This is what I want to do.'" Sarah's advisor helped her find some graduate schools with good limnology programs. "I went to Michigan State University to get a master's degree in applied limnology."

A Big Influence

Sarah's master's degree advisor, Dr. Darrell King, was a big influence on her thinking. "He made me realize possibilities and think seriously about what I could do with my studies. He helped me find the thing that I really wanted to do. It was the turning point in my life." Sarah, as Dr. King's research assistant, worked on advanced wastewater treatments using natural processes. This work paid her a salary while in graduate school and launched her into the work she does today.

After getting her master's, Sarah worked at the Illinois Natural History Survey doing ecological studies on cooling lakes. Cooling lakes are created when hot water used by a power plant is released into the lake to cool.

"There was concern about the effect the hot water had on aquatic ecosystems." It was here that Sarah met Ted, a fishery biologist, whom she married.

When the grant for her work ended, Sarah no longer had a job and wanted to return to graduate school. She and Ted lived near the University of Illinois, her undergraduate school, which didn't have an applied limnology program. However, Sarah learned that the work she really wanted to do was environmental engineering, and Illinois had one of the best graduate programs in this field.

"When I started out in the environmental engineering program, I felt my master's education had already taught me many things that most biologists didn't know. I didn't really think that I needed to know a lot more for my career, but I felt I needed the degree. By the end of my first semester, I had learned more than I'd ever imagined." Sarah still wanted to do applied limnology— problem-solving projects with water quality issues. "I didn't want to be an engineer at first, but I wanted to learn good quantitative skills that engineers know and many biologists don't know. But, by the time I got my Ph.D., I wanted to be an environmental engineer."

Finding the Right Job

After earning her Ph.D., Sarah's first job was assistant professor in the Civil Engineering Department at the University of Houston, Texas, and Ted got a job with the state of Texas. "I had a good teaching experience there, but as a professor you have to have a research program and publish articles about it. I wanted to work with more natural systems, but I had trouble finding people within this university who were interested in the same type of research that I was. So I looked for another university."

Sarah next got a faculty position in the Civil Engineering Department at North Carolina State University (NCSU). Ted got a job with a start-up company. "I fit in at NCSU and got a research program going on natural wastewater treatment systems." During this time Sarah's daughter was born. Sarah didn't get tenure (permanently placed in the job) there, so she had to leave. "Amelia's birth took a lot of my time. But I have no regrets about the decisions I made during that period. I had to choose between spending time to get pub-

lished or spending time with my family, and I haven't regretted one moment that I spent with my family. I know women who can have a family and a tenured academic career, but it's tough for me."

ment three years now; this department suits me very well."

Sarah feels very lucky to have her position. "I enjoy working with graduate students, individually or in small groups. We learn from each

Constructed wetlands are not the natural wetlands but are wetlands built specifically for wastewater treatment.

Sarah didn't have to go far to find another job. When she told a friend in NCSU's Biological and Agricultural Engineering Department that she didn't receive tenure, "He really perked up and said, 'Would you be interested in a job over here?'" Sarah took an assistant professor position. "The position is not permanent, which means we must get grants to fund it. So far, that's not been a problem." Sarah is happy with her job choice. "I've been with this depart-

other. I don't have as much pressure on me as I did in a tenure-track position because I don't do much classroom teaching. This job allows me lots of time to enjoy my family." When she's not working, Sarah likes to walk, and she likes to weave. "But my most favorite thing in the world is doing things with Amelia."

Mary Olson

Mary Olson

Director, Southeast Office, Nuclear Information and
Resource Service, Asheville, NC

Major in Biology

The Perils of Nuclear Power

When asked what she really loves about her work, as director of the Southeast Office of the Nuclear Information and Resource Service (NIRS), Mary Olson replied, "There are two things. As a child, I wanted to help the world and the people, now and in the future. My work makes me feel I'm doing something that not only helps me but helps others and, more importantly, helps future generations."

The second thing Mary loves about her work is meeting and working with wonderful people. "I told a Shoshone (Native American) woman, who was new to this work, that she

Advocate
(A lot of advocacy work is volunteer; salaries depend on size and location of organization)
Entry level average, $24,000 a year
Regional director average, $40,000 a year
Executive director, $50,000 and up a year

MARY'S CARGER PATH

Activist parents
▼ encourage
advocacy

Graduates
college

Contaminated by
▼ radiation at Yale
research job

would meet the most wonderful people. She said 'It is the law of the universe.' I didn't understand what she meant, so she explained. 'We're a bit different from you. We don't think the world should be in balance; we believe the world is always going to balance. We believe that uranium, in the ground, is neither positive nor negative. But when people dig it up, it becomes more negative as it comes to the surface. When put in a nuclear reactor, it becomes the most negative. This requires a long-term response from the universe; but the immediate, short-term response is for many wonderful people to become involved and be the positive to balance this negative.' So, she told me, it's no accident that all of the people I meet in this work are wonderful."

An Advocator is an Educator

NIRS, which is headquartered in Washington, DC, is the national information and networking center for people concerned about nuclear power, radioactive waste, radiation, and sustainable energy issues. The information NIRS gathers about these subjects covers everything from actions of the White House and Congress to actions of the nuclear power industry to reports by nuclear technology experts. Through its educational programs, NIRS provides people with this information. Through its networking mission, NIRS conducts large organizing campaigns and helps people contact groups that can provide them with the resources they need to learn about

Runs retreat for
▼ environmental
education

Inspired by
▼ book *Nuclear
Madness*

Gets job
▼ with NIRS

nuclear issues affecting them. "We have 1,000 grass-roots organizations in the United States that are NIRS members. Last year, we affiliated with the World Information Service on Energy (WISE) in Europe. So now, we have 12 offices on four continents."

As a NIRS regional director, Mary travels throughout her six-state region to give talks, conduct workshops, and organize meetings with concerned citizens and environmental organizations. "I interact with the general public in meetings about local issues. But, mainly NIRS is a resource for people who are already active in these issues in organizations like the Physicians for Social Responsibility and the Women's International League for Peace and Freedom. Many of these local chapters don't have staff, budget, and someone with

the experience I have. I match individuals and groups with the resources they need to accomplish their goals."

A big part of Mary's role as educator is to give people information so they can understand how nuclear power plants and radioactive waste will affect them and the environment. This may begin with explaining the six-step process for using uranium to fuel nuclear reactors. "Each step has

MARY'S CAREER PATH

Meets Pete at NIX MOX meeting, marries

Becomes NIRS regional director

environmental consequences. Uranium, if inhaled where it is mined, milled, and processed, is about 1,000 times more damaging than an x-ray." For the last step of the process, uranium is formed into rods that are radioactive, but the radiation isn't penetrating because the rods are cov-

heat. The heat boils water, the water becomes steam, and the steam turns a turbine, which produces electricity. It's a big, fancy teapot."

However, Mary further explains, splitting uranium atoms during fueling makes the fragments of the atoms 5 million times more radioactive.

Today young people are overwhelmed by the number of environmental issues to work on. I was "called" by the radiation accident.

ered with a metal that shields the radiation. These rods fuel the reactors. "During the fueling process, uranium atoms are split by neutrons. This generates lots of energy that becomes

"When the used rods, which are now waste, are removed from the reactor they are very hot. If you don't cool this highly radioactive waste, it will melt itself and cause a bad accident." The waste is placed in a fuel pool for five years to cool it. "It can be put it into dry containers after five years. These containers are still at the reactor sites."

There are proposals to temporarily store this radioactive waste at a Native American reservation in Utah or to store it at Yucca Mountain, Nevada, where a permanent storage facility is being considered. "We're unhappy about Yucca Mountain because there are two fault lines running through the storage area, and there have been 600 earthquakes measuring over 2.5 since a study of this site was begun." Mary noted that this waste is still 3 million times more radioactive than the original rods, even after the five-year cooling period.

"Of all the nuclear waste generated, over 80 percent of the volume and over 95 percent of the radioactivity come from commercial, nuclear-powered reactors used to generate electricity. The weapons complex and all industrial applications, research, and medicine together have only 5 percent of the radioactivity. Radiation endangers our

CAREER CHECKLIST ✔

You'll like this job if you ...

- Like people

- Can listen to people and understand their concerns

- Want to explain complex technical issues so nontechnical people understand them

- Are concerned about the effects of nuclear power

- Are committed to making the planet safer

- Can put your concerns and commitment ahead of making a big salary

genetic structures. For the individual, this spells cancer; for the species, this spells extinction. What helps me get out of bed every morning is that most of the radioactivity from this waste has not been released into the environment; we still have the opportunity to see that it is never released."

Working to "NIX MOX"

Mary's current project, NIX (reject) MOX, is to educate people about a joint effort by nuclear firms to create and use a fuel made from plutonium that comes from dismantled nuclear weapons and that can be mixed with uranium to power nuclear reactors. MOX stands for Mixed-Oxide Fuel and is the name of this mixture.

Unlike uranium, which occurs naturally in the earth, plutonium is not mined; it's formed in the reactor. "There are two kinds of uranium. The one that neutrons split and that makes heat in the reactor is called U-235. A second uranium in the fuel is called U-238. Neutrons also hit U-238, but its atoms don't split. Sometimes the neutrons bounce off, but if one gets absorbed by the U-238 atom, the atom goes through a fundamental change and becomes plutonium."

Mary notes that designers of nuclear weapons decided to purify one of the four types of plutonium, Plutonium-239, to make weapons-grade plutonium. "Plutonium-239 is more concentrated than what initially comes from the reactor. It has never been used as a reactor fuel." But, to create MOX, Plutonium-239 will be trucked from weapons depots in the West to processing plants built in the Southeast, where it will be mixed with uranium. The MOX fuel will then be trucked to commercial nuclear reactors in the Southeast, where it will fuel the reactors and become high-level radioactive waste. "One big concern is that Plutonium-239 is suited for weapons—to explode. Uranium has some characteristics that allow the operators to control the reactor—the hotter the reactor core gets, the harder it is to split the uranium atom. Plutonium-239 is the opposite."

Mary educates the public about alternatives to MOX fuel. "We know that there are no alternatives for some things. If you need an x-ray and you agree to it, you have been informed and given a chance to consent. However, there are other ways to generate electricity, and people should be informed about them."

Parents Were Educators and Activists

"As a girl, the overwhelming message I got was that the world has lots of challenges, and my job as an adult would be to take on a big issue and do my best to advocate for it." Mary learned about peaceful methods for conflict resolution from her mother. "She used the United Nations as a model for peaceful conflict resolution. She would assign my sister and me the name of a country so we could resolve our fights like countries at the U.N."

Growing up, Mary spent some time in Mount Carroll, Illinois, when her father taught at a small college. She went through school in West Lafayette, Indiana, where her father taught at Purdue University. She entered Reed College, in Oregon, early. "I majored in biology, which was my father's discipline." Mary also spent one year at St. John's College in Santa Fe, New Mexico. "They have a Great Books program there. It influenced my perspective about considering alternatives, rather than accepting current practices. My work today is to be an advocate for people who are challenging current practices." Mary also did theater in college. "This helped with my public speaking."

In college, Mary determined "I wanted to be able to translate techni-

cal scientific information for people who would be affected by it. I decided my biology degree would be worthwhile if I could help people in this way." After graduating, Mary knew she didn't want to do research science, but when she needed work, she got a job as a biomedical research assistant at Yale University Medical School.

Exposed Accidentally to Radiation

At Yale, Mary and other researchers were using radioactive material in their work. "A small petri dish that someone had used for highly radioactive material had not been marked for that and was handed to me. Since it wasn't marked with warning symbols, I didn't know that it was highly radioactive, so I was unknowingly exposed to radiation for a week with no protection. I was contaminated." This was an accident resulting from human error. "The system for safety failed easily when one person didn't mark a little dish." Mary started having health problems based on immune system malfunctions, which she'd never had before. "I attribute them to this radiation exposure."

Mary left research work and moved to Michigan to operate Circle Pines Center, a retreat and conference center and children's camp for environmental education. "My father had been on staff there. I went there as a girl." Mary's work at Circle Pines built the skills she uses to be an effective educator and organizer for NIRS.

When Mary started receiving mail from NIRS, she learned about the nonprofit organization's mission and current projects. She started volunteering for NIRS. There was no local project, so she decided to use her vacation time and her own money to travel to Washington, DC, to help out at NIRS headquarters. "I knew this was the type work that would fulfill my childhood wish. It took about a year and a half before NIRS employed me full time. I had organized their office for them, and they were so impressed that they created a funded position for me, and I moved to Washington."

During her first year at NIRS, Mary noticed that handwritten faxes were coming from Dr. Helen Caldicott, who was asking NIRS for updates on nuclear activity. Mary recognized the well-known physician and author because she had read her book, *Nuclear Madness*. "It was one of the few books about radiation that made sense to me. Dr. Caldicott met with world leaders about the health hazards of radiation. She may have contributed to ending the Cold War. She's a real hero to me."

"Nobody wanted to take time to respond, so I wrote her briefing papers. A year later, she sent me her manuscript for an update to *Nuclear Madness*. She asked me to review it. She had taken my briefing papers and put them into her book. She gave me first acknowledgment."

NIRS's Only Regional Office

When Mary was in Augusta, Georgia, working on NIX MOX, her boss asked her to talk with Pete, who had been on the NIRS mailing list for ten years, just like Mary, and was coming to his first meeting. Mary and Pete talked and corresponded. That was February; they married in November. "I told my boss he had a choice. He could accept my resignation because I was moving to get married, or he could open a regional office. He paused for 30 seconds, then said 'I guess I'm going to open a regional office.'"

Mary became a "new Mom" when she married Pete. Her stepson, Cyrus, is 16. Her stepdaughter, Valerie, is 21. "Cyrus has a huge interest in nuclear issues. Valerie is a fashion model with the Ford Modeling Agency."

Mary's been doing her job for ten years. She works at home and travels usually by car, bus, and plane to speak at meetings and hold workshops. "I'm on the computer and on the phone, so I can do my job no matter where I am."

Getting Started On Your

Own Career Path

Getting Started On
Your Own Career Path

WHAT TO DO NOW

To help you prepare for a career as an environmentalist, the women interviewed for this book recommend things you can do now, while still in school.

SUSTAINABLE FORESTRY AND AGRICULTURE, ROBIN SEARS

Do what you love, so your daily work is something you love to do. I love to be outdoors. Be passionate; this isn't about money. The rewards come from doing what you love.

Be aware of what's happening to the area around you, the state of farmlands and forests and parks. Ask questions and look for answers.

Don't be afraid to try new things and go new places; be adventuresome.

ENDANGERED SPECIES, MARY JAYNE CHURCHILL

Read and learn as much as you can about as many different wildlife species as possible.

When you're near water, walk along the shore or rent a boat to study the wildlife there. Visit farms and zoos, even natural history museums.

Volunteer; there may be a place or a wildlife rehabilitation person in your area who takes in injured or orphaned wild animals.

CLEAN AIR, CHRISTI THEIS

Don't be afraid of science. Everyone can learn it. It is the basis for getting into new technology, opening your thoughts to the future.

Practice good people skills, because you will work with so many different types of people—different backgrounds, different company cultures. To be able to read people, understand them, and communicate with them is essential. You can't get anywhere if you can't get your ideas across and understand theirs.

I highly recommend forcing yourself to give lots of presentations before groups of people.

ECOSYSTEMS, CHRISTINA URANOWSKI

Try to decide what you want to do, what you'll enjoy doing for the rest of your life early in life. When you've decided, get practical experience through volunteering while you're still in school.

The biological career that sounds exciting may not appeal to you when you get in the field. There are neat critters like spiders and snakes in the woods, and you'll get dirty. Field work, volunteering, and internships are great ways to get your feet wet to see if you really like the work. If you don't like the field, you can prepare yourself to do research in the lab.

Find a good mentor, and don't be afraid to ask questions.

RENEWABLE ENERGY, DEBBIE LEWIS

Study more than your small area of interest in math and science. Take sociology courses to help you understand how to work with all types of people, and take public speaking courses so you can communicate your ideas to others.

As you take classes in high school and college to become an engineer, you'll find that engineering is still a man's world. Don't ever flirt with them—just do your job, and they will respect you.

You're going to make mistakes, and, because you're a woman, you're probably going to cry; just try not to do it in front of the men. I've found the men I worked with in math and science to be very sensitive, good people.

Always maintain an impeccable integrity and keep secrets, don't gossip.

GREEN TECHNOLOGIES AND PRODUCTS, ANN BAUMAN

This field is for people who want to help others. Look for environmental groups that are working on clean air, green construction, and visit meetings or join.

Read about toxins, do research at the library and on the Web. Job-shadow someone in toxin research at your local college. Some colleges now offer courses on indoor air quality.

Attend events sponsored by environmental quality groups like the Sierra Club; health associations like the American Lung Association; and government agencies like the Environmental Protection Agency.

ORGANIC, PESTICIDE-FREE FARMING, SUSAN HOUGHTON

Study biology to acquire leaf and insect identification skills. You will need math skills. Study chemistry so you understand how plants grow. Database management courses will help you acquire skills you'll need to manage all aspects of a farm.

Start your own garden if possible. To learn about companion planting (planting different types of plants that like to share the soil together in the same area), read *Carrots Love Tomatoes* by Louise Riotte.

In college take greenhouse management to learn about timing for environmental controls and variety information. Marketing courses will give you skills to help you decide how, where, and to whom you are going to sell your product. Many colleges offer sustainable agriculture courses, and the University of California, Santa Cruz, offers organic farming courses. Internships are offered on some organic farms

TOXIC CLEAN-UP, STEPHANIE SHAKOFSKY

Study chemistry, physics, and math, which is the language of science. Work hard. Don't let anyone tell you that you can't do something. Continue asking questions until you understand.

Become involved in community service. Go to civic meetings. Watch what civic leaders do. Work at the local level, but understand how the planet works.

FOREST HEALTH PROTECTION, DONNA LEONARD

Explore your local area for insects. Learn about their behavior and habitats; you can find lots of information in your library.

Prepare to get a college degree. It can be in a broad range of subjects related to biology. Forestry is probably the most common, but we have fewer foresters now, more ecology-related degrees like conservation biology, watershed experts, wildlife managers, natural resources, and entomology.

WASTE MANAGEMENT, SARAH LIEHR

Finding what I wanted to do has been a wandering process for me. I didn't focus on one thing and hold to it. You can follow your instincts, like I did. Use the library and Web to wander through different environmental fields until you find something that fits with what you love to do.

If you're focused on a specific career, use the library and Web to learn about it. Join groups involved in the area you want to pursue. When you go for your degrees, don't get a Ph.D. just because you think you'll make more money; be sure it is something you really want to do.

ADVOCACY, MARY OLSON

Every experience you have in life will be useful in whatever advocacy work you chose. Any activity you pursue will contribute to your work.

Books and the Web are not the only good sources of information. People are a great resource, so also do research by asking people questions.

RECOMMENDED READING

Magazines and other publications covering the environmental fields are varied and plentiful, many published by environmental groups. Many of the books listed below are recommended by *Best Books for Young Adult Readers*, edited by Stephen Calvert.

Fiction

Ancient One by T. A. Barron. (1992). Putnam. (Kate fights to save a stand of Oregon redwoods in this time-travel fantasy)

California Blue by David Klass. (1994). Scholastic. (Boy finds butterfly chrysalis that turns out to be an unknown species)

Circle Within a Circle by Monte Killingsworth. (1994). Macmillan/Margaret K. McElderry. (Runaway teenage boy and Chinook Indian join a crusade to save sacred land from development)

Cry of the Wolf by Melvin Burgess. (1992). Morrow/Tambourine. (Hunter sets out to wipe out last pack of wolves in England)

Fire Bug Connection by Jean Craighead George. (1993). Harper Collins. (Teen mystery in which Maggie tries to figure out which environmental factor is killing Czech fire bugs)

Forest by Janet Taylor Lisle. (1993). Orchard. (Satire: 12-year-old girl and squirrel battle adults who are thoughtless about the environment)

Giving Tree and *Where the Sidewalk Ends* by Shel Silverstein. (1964 & 1974). NY: Harper & Row. (Includes two classic "trash" poems)

Kelsey's Raven by Sylvia Peck. (1992). Morrow. (Old, injured raven is adopted by a family and changes their lives)

The Lorax by Dr. Seuss; also available in sound recording. Random House. (Challenging polluters)

The Missing 'Gator of Gumbo Limbo: An Ecological Mystery by Jean

Craighead George. (1992). (Girl and her mother scheme to protect an Everglades alligator threatened by armed official)

Shadowmaker by Joan Lowery Nixon. (1994). (When Katie's journalist mother probes into toxic waste dumping, Katie discovers events at her school are related)

Violators by Gunnard Landers. (1991). Walker. (Undercover agent for U.S. Fish & Wildlife Service must bring poachers to justice)

Whalesinger by Welwyn Wilton Katz. (1991). Macmillan/Margaret K. McElderry. (Two Canadian teens spending the summer on the California coast encounter a corrupt research scientist, endangered whales, and natural disasters)

Nonfiction

Air Pollution by Kathlyn Gay. (1991). Watts. (Examines ecological effects and health risks of atmospheric pollution and outlines ways to fight it)

Books by Rachel Carson: *Silent Spring, The Sea Around Us, Under the Sea Wind, The Edge of the Sea.*

Carrots Love Tomatoes by Louise Riotta. (1998). Pownal, UT: Storey Publishing.

Choices for Our Future by Ocean Robbins & Sol Solomon. (1994). Summerton, TN: Book Publishing. (Founders of Youth for Environmental Sanity believe young people have influence)

50 Simple Things Kids Can Do to Recycle. (1994). EarthWorks Press. (Lists home and school projects and how to handle certain materials)

Global Garbage: Exporting Trash and Toxic Waste by Kathlyn Gay. (1992). Watts. (Documents many ways humans have polluted earth and outer space)

Math Book for Girls and Other Beings Who Count by Valerie Wyatt. (2000). Buffalo, NY: Kids Can Press.

National Audubon Society Almanac of the Environment: The Ecology of Everyday Life by Valerie Harms. (1994). Putnam. (Ecology of the body, home, community, ocean, land, and the complex politics of environmentalism)

Nuclear Madness by Helen Caldicott. ISBN 0-393-03947-1. W.W. Norton.

Spill: The Story of the Exxon Valdez by Terry Carr. (1991). Watts.

(Straightforward account of one of the worst ecological disasters of our time)

Biographies

John Muir: Wilderness Protector by Ginger Wadsworth. (1992). Lerner.

Kate Sessions, Pioneer Horticulturist by Elizabeth MacPhail. San Diego Historical Society.

Rachel Carson: The Environmental Movement by John Henricksson. (1991). New Directions.

Walking with the Great Apes: Jane Goodall, Dian Fossey, Birute Goldikas by Sy Montgomery. (1991). Houghton Mifflin.

Window on the Deep: The Adventures of Underwater Explorer Sylvia Earle by Andrea Conley. (1991). New England Aquarium Books.

Reference

Conservation Directory, published annually by the National Wildlife Federation, Reston, VA. (Lists conservation groups, agencies, and universities and colleges that offer environmental courses)

General References

Career Information Center (7th ed.). (1999). Macmillan.

Encyclopedia of Career and Vocational Guidance. (2000). Chicago: J. G. Ferguson

The Girls' Guide to Life: How to Take Charge of the Issues That Affect You by Catherine Dee. (1997). Boston: Little, Brown & Co. (Celebrates achievements of girls and women, extensive resources)

Peterson's Scholarships, Grants, and Prizes. (1997). Princeton, NJ: Peterson's; Web site: www.petersons.com

THE INTERNET

There are many Web sites that will give you historic and up-to-date information about the environment. Several sites list environmental programs and the many types of jobs that support them. Some sites list current job openings. We name a few of these sites below.

JOB SITES

• http://environmental-jobs.com — Environmental Careers World, 100 Bridge Street, Bldg C, Hampton, VA 23669, (757) 727-7895

• www.ecojobs.com — Environmental Careers Organization, 179 South St., Boston, MA 02111, (617) 426-4375

• www.epa.gov — U.S. Environmental Protection Agency, Washington, DC; also your state department of natural resources

• www.ets.uidaho.edu/winr/ — Women in Natural Resources publish a quarterly journal and a monthly job flyer which is also online. University of Idaho, P.O. Box 441114, Moscow, ID 83844-1114

MISCELLANEOUS

• www.deenaloveland.com — Real estate professional Deena Loveland, who has built an earth-friendly home, created this site so you can see the progress, learn about the techniques, and view the final product of her "house of the Millennium" in Washington state.

• www.womenoceanographers.org — This site, sponsored by the Woods Hole Oceanographic Institute in Massachusetts, profiles women's jobs in the marine field.

ORGANIZATIONS

Professional Organizations

There are many special interest organizations and groups that serve those interested in protecting the environment. Many have informative Web sites. Below, we list the engineering and science professions especially geared to women and some well-known environmental groups that have educational programs for young people.

THE ASSOCIATION FOR WOMEN IN SCIENCE

AWIS is dedicated to achieving equity and full participation for women in science, mathematics, engineering, and technology. Among its activities are mentoring programs.

1200 New York Ave., NW, Ste. 650, Washington, DC 20005

(202) 326-8940

Web site: www.awis.org

AWSEM – WITI

Advocates for Women in Science, Engineering, and Mathematics (AWSEM) and Women in Technology International (WITI) have teamed up to create a girls' advocacy program linking girls with science and technology professionals.

20000 NW Walker Rd., Beaverton, OR 97006

(503) 748-1504

Web site: www.awsem.com/witi.html

WOMEN IN TECHNOLOGY INTERNATIONAL AND WITI FOUNDATION

6345 Balboa Blvd., Encino, CA 91316

Web site: www.witi.com

SOCIETY OF WOMEN ENGINEERS

Offers certificate and scholarship programs.

120 Wall St., 11th Floor, New York, NY 10005

(212) 509-9257

Web site: www.swe.org

JETS, INC.

Junior Engineering Technical Society offers broad range of brochures, books, and videos. Provides competitions and events for high school students.

1420 King St., Ste. 405, Alexandria, VA 22314-2794

(703) 548-5387, or email: jets@nae.edu

Web site: www.asee.org/external/jets/

NATIONAL ACADEMY OF ENGINEERING

Has a special program, the Celebration of Women in Engineering. Check their Web site at www.nae.edu/cwe.

2101 Constitution Avenue, NW, Washington, DC 20418

(202) 334 1605

Web site: www.nae.edu

Environmental Organizations

ECOLOGICAL SOCIETY OF AMERICA

1707 H Street, NW, Ste. 400, Washington, DC 20006

(202) 833-8773

Web site: www.sdsc.edu/~esa/esa.html

NATIONAL WILDLIFE FEDERATION

Has educational program for all ages, publishes *Ranger Rick* magazine and the annual *Conservation Directory*.

11100 Wildlife Center Dr., Reston, VA 20190-5362

(703) 438-6000

Web site: www.nwf.org

ORGANIC FARMING RESEARCH FOUNDATION

Advocates for strong standards and sponsors research to improve organic farming practices.

P.O. Box 440, Santa Cruz, CA 95061

(831) 426-6606

Web site: www.ofrf.org

SIERRA CLUB

Has a Youth in Wilderness Program which raises money and delivers grants supporting all types of youth outdoor activities from outdoor field trips to special camps focusing on wilderness educational activities.

85 Second St., Second Floor, San Francisco, CA 94105-3441

(415) 977-5500

Web site: www.sierraclub.org

WORLDWATCH INSTITUTE

This organization is dedicated to objective research and dispersing environmental information. Worldwatch produces many reports and publications, among them a yearly state-of-the-world book, reporting on current status of environmental issues around the globe.

1776 Massachusetts Ave., NW, Washington, DC 20036-1904

(202) 452-1999

Web site: www.worldwatch.org

How COOL Are You?!

Cool girls like to DO things, not just sit around like couch potatoes. There are many things you can get involved in now to benefit your future. Some cool girls even know what careers they want (or think they want).

Not sure what you want to do? That's fine, too… the Cool Careers series can help you explore lots of careers with a number of great, easy to use tools! Learn where to go and to whom you should talk about different careers, as well as books to read and videos to see. Then, you're on the road to cool girl success!

Written especially for girls, this new series tells what it's like today for women in all types of jobs with special emphasis on nontraditional careers for women. The upbeat and informative pages provide answers to questions you want answered, such as:

- ✔ **What jobs do women find meaningful?**
- ✔ **What do women succeed at today?**
- ✔ **How did they prepare for these jobs?**
- ✔ **How did they find their job?**
- ✔ **What are their lives like?**
- ✔ **How do I find out more about this type of work?**

Each book profiles ten women who love their work. These women had dreams, but didn't always know what they wanted to be when they grew up. Zoologist Claudia Luke knew she wanted to work outdoors and that she was interested in animals, but she didn't even know what a zoologist was, much less what they did and how you got to be one. Elizabeth Gruben was going to be a lawyer until she discovered the world of Silicon Valley computers and started her own multimedia company. Mary Beth Quinn grew up in Stowe, Vermont, where she skied competitively and taught skiing. Now she runs a ski school at a Virginia ski resort. These three women's stories appear with others in a new series of career books for young readers.

The Cool Careers for Girls series encourages career exploration and broadens girls' career horizons. It shows girls what it takes to succeed, by providing easy-to-read information about careers that young girls may not have considered because they didn't know about them. They learn from women who are in today's workplace—women who know what it takes today to get the job.

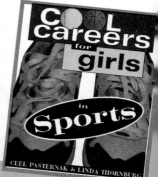

EACH BOOK ALSO INCLUDES:

✔ A personality checklist for each job
✔ Lists of books to read and videos to see
✔ Salary information
✔ Supportive organizations to contact for scholarships, mentoring, or apprenticeship and intern programs

THE BOOKS ALSO LOOK AT:

✔ What skills are needed to succeed in each career
✔ The physical demands of the different jobs
✔ What the women earn
✔ How to judge whether you have the personality traits to succeed in the different jobs
✔ How much leisure time you'll have
✔ How women balance work and relationships
✔ Reasons for changing jobs
✔ The support received by women to pursue their goals
✔ How women handle pregnancy and child care
✔ What you need to study to get these jobs and others

So GET WITH IT!
Start your **Cool Careers for Girls** library today...

ORDER FORM

TITLE	PAPER	CLOTH	QUANTITY
Cool Careers for Girls in Computers	$12.95	$19.95	_____
Cool Careers for Girls in Sports	$12.95	$19.95	_____
Cool Careers for Girls with Animals	$12.95	$19.95	_____
Cool Careers for Girls in Health	$12.95	$19.95	_____
Cool Careers for Girls in Engineering	$12.95	$19.95	_____
Cool Careers for Girls in Food	$12.95	$19.95	_____
Cool Careers for Girls in Construction	$12.95	$19.95	_____
Cool Careers for Girls in Performing Arts	$12.95	$19.95	_____
Cool Careers for Girls in Air and Space	$12.95	$19.95	_____
Cool Careers for Girls in Law	$12.95	$19.95	_____
Cool Careers for Girls as Environmentalists	$12.95	$19.95	_____
Cool Careers for Girls as Crime Solvers	$12.95	$19.95	_____

SUBTOTAL _____

VA Residents add 4½% sales tax _____
Shipping/handling $5.00+ $5.00
$1.50 for each additional book order (__ x $1.50) _____

TOTAL ENCLOSED _____

SHIP TO: (street address only for UPS or RPS delivery)
Name: _____
Address: _____

❏ I enclose check/money order for $ _____ made payable to Impact Publications
❏ Charge $ _____ to: ❏ Visa ❏ MasterCard ❏ AmEx ❏ Discover

Card #: _____   Expiration: _____
Signature: _____   Phone number: _____

Phone toll-free at 1-800/361-1055, or fax/mail/email your order to:
IMPACT PUBLICATIONS   9104 Manassas Drive, Suite N, Manassas Park, VA 20111-5211
Fax: 703/335-9486; email: orders@impactpublications.com

EAU CLAIRE DISTRICT LIBRARY